CONTENTS

Useful information for readers

Dear Reader,

Issues: Teenage Conceptions

The UK currently has the highest rate of teenage pregnancies in western Europe — seven times those of the Netherlands and double those of France or Germany. Why is the rate so high, and how can it best be tackled? This book looks at teen conceptions and their outcomes in the UK, the challenges faced by young parents and at strategies for preventing high rates of teenage pregnancy in future.

The purpose of *Issues*

Teenage Conceptions is the one hundred and eighty-second volume in the **Issues** series. The aim of this series is to offer up-to-date information about important issues in our world. Whether you are a regular reader or new to the series, we do hope you find this book a useful overview of the many and complex issues involved in the topic. This title replaces an older volume in the **Issues** series, Volume 133: **Teen Pregnancy and Lone Parents,** which is now out of print.

Titles in the **Issues** series are resource books designed to be of especial use to those undertaking project work or requiring an overview of facts, opinions and information on a particular subject, particularly as a prelude to undertaking their own research.

The information in this book is not from a single author, publication or organisation; the value of this unique series lies in the fact that it presents information from a wide variety of sources, including:
- ⇨ Government reports and statistics
- ⇨ Newspaper articles and features
- ⇨ Information from think-tanks and policy institutes
- ⇨ Magazine features and surveys
- ⇨ Website material
- ⇨ Literature from lobby groups and charitable organisations.*

Critical evaluation

Because the information reprinted here is from a number of different sources, readers should bear in mind the origin of the text and whether the source is likely to have a particular bias or agenda when presenting information (just as they would if undertaking their own research). It is hoped that, as you read about the many aspects of the issues explored in this book, you will critically evaluate the information presented. It is important that you decide whether you are being presented with facts or opinions. Does the writer give a biased or an unbiased report? If an opinion is being expressed, do you agree with the writer?

Teenage Conceptions offers a useful starting point for those who need convenient access to information about the many issues involved. However, it is only a starting point. Following each article is a URL to the relevant organisation's website, which you may wish to visit for further information.

Kind regards,

Lisa Firth
Editor, **Issues** series

** Please note that Independence Publishers has no political affiliations or opinions on the topics covered in the **Issues** series, and any views quoted in this book are not necessarily those of the publisher or its staff.*

ISSUES TODAY
A RESOURCE FOR KEY STAGE 3

Younger readers can also benefit from the thorough editorial process which characterises the **Issues** series with our resource books for 11- to 14-year-old students, **Issues Today**. In addition to containing information from a wide range of sources, rewritten with this age group in mind, **Issues Today** titles also feature comprehensive glossaries, an accessible and attractive layout and handy tasks and assignments which can be used in class, for homework or as a revision aid. In addition, these titles are fully photocopiable. For more information, please visit our website (www.independence. co.uk).

Teenagers: sexual behaviour and pregnancy

Information from the fpa

Sexual behaviour

The second National Survey of Sexual Attitudes and Lifestyles (Natsal 2000), which included over 11,000 men and women aged 16 to 44 in Great Britain,[1] found that:

⇨ the average (median) age at first heterosexual intercourse was 16 for both men and women;

⇨ nearly a third of men and a quarter of women aged 16 to 19 had heterosexual intercourse before they were 16;

⇨ about 80 per cent of young people aged 16 to 24 said that they had used a condom when they first had sex;

⇨ less than one in ten had used no contraception at all when they first had sex;

⇨ one in five young men and nearly half of young women aged 16 to 24 said they wished they had waited longer to start having sex. They were twice as likely to say this if they had been under 15 when they first had sex;

⇨ both young men and women aged 16 to 24 had had an average of three heterosexual partners in their lifetime;[1]

⇨ about one per cent (0.9 per cent men, 1.6 per cent women) of 16- to 24-year-olds had had one or more new same-sex partners in the previous year.[2]

Natsal 2000 did not include Northern Ireland. A separate survey carried out in 2000 by fpa in Northern Ireland and the University of Ulster included over 1,000 young people aged 14 to 25.[3] It found that:

⇨ the average (median) age at first heterosexual intercourse was 15.6 years (14.9 for men and 15.9 for women);

⇨ just over a third had experienced sexual intercourse before 17 (the legal age of consent in Northern Ireland) and a quarter had sex before 16;

⇨ nearly two-thirds (63.8 per cent) had used a condom when they first had sex, either alone or with another method of contraception;

⇨ about a quarter had used no contraception at all when they first had sex;

⇨ just under a third (31.6 per cent) said they felt they had sex too early, and this was more likely (43 per cent) if they had been under 16 at the time;

⇨ on average, the sexually active 14- to 25-year-olds had had six sexual partners; the average for young women was five, and young men eight.

Use of contraception

An Office for National Statistics (ONS) survey[4] of women aged 16 to 49 in Great Britain found that among 16- to 19-year-olds in 2007–08:

⇨ 56 per cent said they used contraception;

⇨ among these, almost equal numbers said they used the pill or condoms (some will use both);

⇨ 86 per cent had heard of emergency hormonal contraception (EHC);

⇨ seven per cent had used EHC and one per cent the emergency IUD at least once in the previous 12 months.

There is no equivalent survey data on contraceptive usage by teenagers in Northern Ireland. The following statistics relate only to women attending community family planning clinics in 2003–04.[5]

⇨ 49 per cent of women aged 16–19 were using the pill and 21 per cent the condom as their main method of contraception.

⇨ Although women under 20 accounted for 31 per cent of all EHC provided through family planning clinics in Northern Ireland, only four per cent of the overall total was those aged under 16.

Use of contraceptive clinic services

⇨ 78,000 women aged under 16 attended family planning clinics in England in 2006–07. This

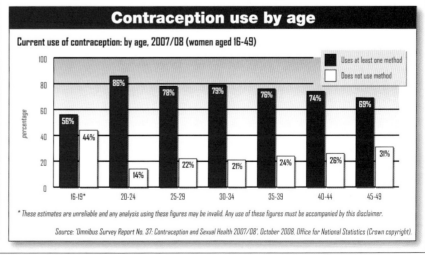

Contraception use by age

Current use of contraception: by age, 2007/08 (women aged 16-49)

- Uses at least one method
- Does not use method

Age	Uses at least one method	Does not use method
16-19*	56%	44%
20-24	86%	14%
25-29	78%	22%
30-34	79%	21%
35-39	76%	24%
40-44	74%	26%
45-49	69%	31%

These estimates are unreliable and any analysis using these figures may be invalid. Any use of these figures must be accompanied by this disclaimer.

Source: 'Omnibus Survey Report No. 37: Contraception and Sexual Health 2007/08', October 2008. Office for National Statistics (Crown copyright).

represented 8.3 per cent of the resident population, a slight decrease from 2006-07.[6]

⇨ 255,000 or 19.6 per cent of the resident female population in England aged 16 to 19 years of age visited a family planning clinic in 2007-08, a slight decrease from 2006-07.[6]

Teenage pregnancy

⇨ The UK has the highest teenage birth and abortion rates in Western Europe.[7]

The UK has the highest teenage birth and abortion rates in Western Europe

---

England[8]
In 2006, there were:
⇨ 39,003 under-18 conceptions, a rate of 40.4 per 1,000 females aged 15 to 17. Nearly half (49 per cent) of the pregnancies were terminated;
⇨ 7,296 under-16 conceptions, a rate of 7.7 per 1,000 females aged 13 to 15. Over half (60 per cent) of the pregnancies were terminated.
Wales[9]
In 2006, there were:
⇨ 2,598 under-18 conceptions, a rate of 44.9 per 1,000 females aged 15 to 17. Over a third (42.6 per cent) of the pregnancies were terminated;
⇨ 496 under-16 conceptions, a rate of 8.6 per 1,000 females aged 13 to 15. Over half (53 per cent) of the pregnancies were terminated.
Scotland[10]
(Unlike England and Wales, Scottish conception data includes miscarriages managed in hospitals as well as registered births and abortions.)
In 2006, there were:
⇨ 3,910 under-18 conceptions, a rate of 41.5 per 1,000 females aged 15 to 17. About 45 per cent of the pregnancies ended in abortion;
⇨ 772 under-16 conceptions, a rate of 8.1 per 1,000 13- to 15-year-olds. Over half (59 per cent) of the pregnancies ended in abortion.
Northern Ireland

⇨ Conception data is not available for Northern Ireland, due to the lack of complete data on the number of women having abortions. Abortion is only legal in Northern Ireland in exceptional circumstances.
⇨ In 2007, 235 teenagers travelled to England to have an abortion,[11] although this number is likely to be an underestimate.
⇨ In 2006, there were 1,427 teenage births (under 20), a rate of 22.5 per 1,000 females aged 15 to 19.[12]

Abortion
England and Wales[11]
⇨ In 2007, 20,289 women aged under 18 had an abortion. Of these, 4,376 were under 16.
⇨ The under-18 abortion rate was 20.0 per 1,000 and the under-16 rate was 4.0.
Scotland[13]
⇨ In 2007, 3,176 women aged 16 to 19 and 372 under-16s had an abortion.
⇨ The abortion rate in 16- to 19-year-olds was 24.5 per 1,000.
Northern Ireland (see Teenage pregnancy section)

References

1 Wellings K et al, 'Sexual behaviour in Britain: early heterosexual experience', *Lancet*, vol 358 (2001), 1843-1850.
2 Johnson A et al, 'Sexual behaviour in Britain: partnerships, practices and HIV risk behaviours', *Lancet*, vol 358 (2001), 1835-1842.
3 Schubotz D et al, *Towards Better Sexual Health: A survey of sexual attitudes and lifestyles of young people in Northern Ireland*. Research report (London: fpa, 2003).
4 Lader D and Hopkins G, *Contraception and Sexual Health, 2007/08* (London: Office for National Statistics, 2008).
5 fpa, *Family Planning Services in Northern Ireland* (Belfast: fpa, 2005).
6 Information Centre, *NHS contraceptive services, England: 2007-08* (London: IC, 2008).
7 UNICEF, *A League Table of Teenage Births in Rich Nations* (Florence: Innocenti Research Centre, 2001).
8 Teenage Pregnancy Unit, *Teenage Conception Statistics for England 1998-2006*.
9 Welsh Assembly Government, Statistical Directorate, *Teenage Conceptions in Wales, 2006*.
10 ISD Scotland, *Teenage Pregnancy Statistics, year ending December 2006*.
11 Department of Health, *Abortion Statistics, England and Wales: 2007* (London: DH, 2008). Statistical Bulletin 2008/01.
12 Northern Ireland Statistics and Research Agency, 'Births', accessed 19 November 2008.
13 ISD Scotland, Abortion.
February 2009

⇨ The above information is an extract from the fpa factsheet *Teenagers: sexual health and behaviour* and is reprinted with permission. Visit www.fpa.org.uk for more information or to view the full factsheet.

© fpa

It didn't mean much when it was just a bunch of statistics!

Conception rate increases among under-18s

Information from the Office for National Statistics

The conception rate among women aged under 18 in England and Wales has risen for the first time since 2002.

There were an estimated 8,196 conceptions to girls aged under 16 in 2007, representing just under one per cent of all conceptions

Provisional figures published today in the Office for National Statistics' journal *Health Statistics Quarterly* show that the under-18 conception rate increased from 40.9 conceptions per 1,000 women aged 15 to 17 in 2006 to 41.9 in 2007. The estimated number of conceptions to women aged under 18 in 2007 was 42,918 and these represented 4.8 per cent of all conceptions in England and Wales.

The under-16 conception rate increased from 7.8 per 1,000 girls aged 13 to 15 in 2006 to 8.3 in 2007. There were an estimated 8,196 conceptions to girls aged under 16 in 2007, representing just under one per cent of all conceptions.

Overall, there were an estimated 894,100 conceptions to women of all ages in England and Wales in 2007, compared with 870,000 in 2006, an increase of 2.8 per cent. Conception rates rose in women of all ages, with the overall rate increasing from 78.3 to 80.3 conceptions per 1,000 women aged 15 to 44.

Women at all ages over 30 years have seen sustained increases in conception rates since 2000. The largest percentage increase in conceptions to women aged over 18 was in the 30- to 34-year-old age group, where the rate rose from 117.5 conceptions per 1,000 women aged 30 to 34 in 2006 to 121.7 in 2007. Conceptions to 30- to 34-year-olds made up 23.6 per cent of all conceptions in 2007, the second largest proportion by age group.

In 2007, the conception rate remained highest for women aged 25 to 29, at 133.4 per 1,000 women in the age group. This age group also had the highest number of conceptions with 234,200 in 2007, making up 26.2 per cent of all conceptions.

As in 2006, 22 per cent of all conceptions in 2007 led to a legal abortion. For women aged under 18, this figure was 50 per cent compared with 48 per cent in 2006.
26 February 2009

⇨ The above information is reprinted with kind permission from the Office for National Statistics. Visit www.statistics.gov.uk for more.
© Crown copyright

Frequently asked questions about pregnancy

Information from AVERT

How does a woman become pregnant?

A woman usually becomes pregnant after having sexual intercourse. This is where a man puts his erect penis inside a woman's vagina. The friction caused by moving his penis in and out of her vagina will cause him to get increasingly excited until eventually he ejaculates (or 'comes') and releases a sticky white substance called semen. This semen contains millions of tiny sperm cells, which then swim up the woman's vagina, into her uterus

AVERTing HIV and AIDS

(womb) and then into her Fallopian tubes where they may join with the tiny egg that she releases from one of her ovaries every month. If this 'joining' (also known as fertilisation or conception) occurs, then she will become pregnant.

How can I prevent pregnancy?

If you don't want to become pregnant, you will need to use contraception. There are lots of different forms of contraception available. The most well known are the contraceptive pill and the condom.

Is there a 'safe time' to have sexual intercourse?

Pregnancy can only occur in the few days following ovulation (the release of an egg). This usually takes place at some point in the middle of a woman's menstrual cycle, between her periods. Unfortunately, women have no definite way of knowing exactly when they are ovulating, so there is no guaranteed 'safe' time to have unprotected sex.

Sperm can survive inside the body for several days while they wait for an egg to be released, and the egg takes several days to travel to the uterus, meaning a woman can potentially become pregnant over quite a long period of time. This is why even unprotected sex during a woman's period can sometimes result in pregnancy. If she has irregular periods (as many girls do in the first few years of menstruation), 'safe' days can be particularly difficult to predict. Some couples do use the so-called 'rhythm' method as a form of contraception (i.e. only having sex on certain days), but the success rate is not high, and it also offers no protection from STDs such as HIV.

What are the chances of becoming pregnant from a single act of sex?

The likelihood of becoming pregnant from a single act of unprotected sex (for example, from a one-night stand) varies from person to person, and also depends on the stage of a woman's menstrual cycle. The probability is highest around the time of ovulation (when the egg is released), when, on average, up to one-third of women will become pregnant from having sex once.

What is the best way to get pregnant?

Many women spend much of their life trying not to get pregnant, and then find that when they actually try to have a baby, it takes longer than they had hoped. If you are trying for a baby and don't get pregnant the first time you try, it is important not to panic. Many perfectly healthy women can take up to a year or more to become pregnant. Though pregnancy is a theoretical possibility any time you have sex, your best chance of getting pregnant will be if you have frequent sex around the time of ovulation. For women with a regular 28-day menstrual cycle, this will be approximately 14 days after the start of their last period, although it can vary from woman to woman. In some countries it may be possible to buy an ovulation testing kit from a chemist to help you work out when you're most fertile.

If you continue to have problems, you should contact your doctor for advice. They will be able to refer you for tests to ensure that there are no physical problems that are preventing you from conceiving.

If a man pulls his penis out before he comes or doesn't put it in all the way, can a woman still get pregnant?

Unfortunately, even if a man doesn't insert his penis all the way, or withdraws his penis before ejaculation, a woman can still become pregnant. This is because 'pre-come' (the

lubricating fluid that leaks out of a man's penis before and during sex) can contain sperm. If this fluid gets in or around a woman's vagina, it can find its way inside, and she can become pregnant.

Can a woman become pregnant as a result of anal sex?

A woman cannot become pregnant as a result of anal sex directly, although if any sperm leaks from the anus and enters the vagina, pregnancy could occur. Anal sex is therefore not the best way of avoiding pregnancy on a long-term basis. It is better to use regular contraception such as the birth control pill or condoms.

The first sign of pregnancy is usually the absence of a period

---

Anyone wanting to try anal intercourse should be 100 per cent sure that their partner is willing too, as the idea of anal sex makes many people very uncomfortable. It also carries a higher risk of transmission for HIV and other infections, so it is a good idea to use a condom if you do decide to try it.

Can a woman become pregnant through oral sex if she swallows sperm?

No, a woman cannot become pregnant as a result of oral sex even if she swallows. A woman can only become pregnant if sperm get inside her vagina.

Can sperm pass through clothes?

No, generally clothing acts as a barrier against sperm.

Are there any ways to tell if you are pregnant without using a pregnancy test?

The first sign of pregnancy is usually the absence of a period. Other symptoms of pregnancy can include tender breasts, nausea and tiredness, but not everybody experiences these. If you suspect you are pregnant you should take a pregnancy test. This can

... REMEMBER HOW WE AVOIDED TALKING ABOUT GETTING PREGNANT...?

be done at a clinic, or you can buy a home testing kit from most major supermarkets and pharmacies. If you use a home test kit it is important to get the result confirmed by your doctor or healthcare professional at a local clinic.

How long should I wait before carrying out a pregnancy test?

It depends on the type of test you buy. Most tests recommend testing on the day your period is due, although you can buy some that can detect the pregnancy hormone in your urine up to four or five days before this. Make sure you read the instructions thoroughly to find out how long you should wait. If you are not sure when your period is due, the best idea is to wait for at least ten days after having had unprotected sex before testing (although it is worth remembering that it can take up to 19 days or more to show a positive result). If you get a negative result but your period still doesn't arrive, you should test again at three-day intervals, until your period starts or you get a positive result. The

sooner you find out you are pregnant, the sooner you can start thinking about what to do next.

The test result was negative, but my period still hasn't arrived. Could I still be pregnant?

If you have tested too soon (see above), then yes, you might still be pregnant. However, if you are sure you haven't tested too soon, then it may well be stress that has delayed your period. Worrying about pregnancy (or anything else) can drive your stress hormones up, and this can in turn interfere with your menstrual cycle. If you have lost or gained a lot of weight recently, have undertaken lots of vigorous exercise or you have irregular periods generally, these could also be to blame. Girls who have only recently started their periods often experience very irregular cycles too, so if you've only been menstruating for a couple of years or less, try not to panic! If your period is more than a week or two late when you're normally regular,

however, you should probably think about seeing your doctor.

I'm pregnant! What can I do?

If you were planning to get pregnant, then finding out you're expecting a baby can be a wonderful surprise. However, if you weren't, it is more likely to be a big shock. The most important thing to remember is that you are not alone, and you do have more than one option. The first thing you should do is go to your doctor or your local sexual health or family planning clinic. They will be able to discuss your options with you and help you to decide what to do next. Whether you decide to keep the baby, put it up for adoption or have an abortion (in places where it's legal), it's essential that you do what's right for you and don't feel pressurised into making a decision.

⇨ The above information is reprinted with kind permission from AVERT. Visit www.avert.org for more.
© AVERT

Teenage pregnancy

Information for young people at school

Emergency contraception

If you've had sex within the last couple of days and you think you might be pregnant, you may be able to get emergency contraception (the 'morning after pill') if you contact your doctor, a sexual health clinic or family planning clinic urgently. If you're over 16, you can buy emergency contraception from a chemist, though you will have to pay for it.

Getting a pregnancy test

Your doctor, young person's clinic or youth advice centre will be able to arrange this for you free of charge. The school nurse may also be able to help. You can buy a pregnancy test from a pharmacy or the bigger supermarkets, but you will have to pay about £8-12.

Your right to privacy

Your visit will be in confidence and they will not tell your parents or teachers

that you have been there or the results of the test unless you ask them to.

Doctors, nurses and other health workers are obliged by law to give you the same right to privacy and confidentiality as adults, even if you are under 16.

They will only pass on information about your visit if they think you are in danger – even then they should discuss this with you first.

You can find out more about your right to receive confidential advice from the Brook website (www.brook.org.uk).

My test is positive – what should I do?

Tell your parents! If you are worried about this, speak to a teacher or an adult you trust, and ask them for help. Naturally, some parents will be upset or angry at first, but most soon get over this and will do their best to help you.

It's rare for parents to feel so

strongly that they will not support you in any way. But if this happens, your teacher, personal adviser or youth worker will be able to put you in touch with someone who can help.

Doctors, nurses and other health workers are obliged by law to give you the same right to privacy and confidentiality as adults, even if you are under 16

Don't tell the whole class

It may not be a good idea to tell too many of your friends or classmates at this time, especially if you are thinking about having an abortion. Some people have very strong views on this and may not be very kind to you.

I'm not sure if I want to keep the baby

This is a decision only you can make. Your family, friends, the baby's father or his family may want to influence what you do, but the final decision is yours.

If you are thinking about having an abortion, you can get independent advice and information from your doctor, school nurse, clinic or advice centre. You can get advice online or over the phone from:

⇨ British Pregnancy Advisory Service (www.bpas.org.uk);
⇨ Brook (www.brook.org.uk).

It is best if abortions are carried out as early in the pregnancy as possible and if it has been more than 12 weeks since your last period, it may be difficult or even impossible to arrange.

Adoption

If you want to go through with the pregnancy but are thinking about having the baby adopted you will need to talk to a social worker before the baby is born.

Will my boyfriend get into trouble?

Your boyfriend is much more likely to get into trouble if you are under 16 and he is much older than you are, or if he forced you or tricked you into having sex with him.

The Family Planning Association has a useful page about UK law relating to sexual behaviour (www. fpa.org.uk).

I have decided to keep the baby. What next?

You will need to see your doctor or a midwife. He or she will confirm the pregnancy and will be able to tell you when the baby is due. They will also arrange for you to see a midwife and maybe to have a scan at the hospital. It is important for you and your baby that you keep any appointments arranged for you during your pregnancy. Smoking and drinking alcohol can be very bad for your baby's development and health, as can any kind of drug. It is best to check with the doctor or midwife before taking medicines of any kind.

Will I still have to go to school?

You will still be expected to go to school up to the normal school leaving age (end of Year 11) both during your pregnancy and after the birth of your baby.

You will need to tell a senior teacher as soon as possible to plan for your education during your pregnancy. They can look at any problems or difficulties you are having and see if there are ways they can make your time at school during the pregnancy any easier.

It may be possible to alter or reduce your timetable as you get further into your pregnancy and you will probably get some home tuition for the few weeks just before and just after the baby is born.

You will be allowed to take time off for any hospital and doctor appointments, but if you are not well enough to attend school for more than a few days because of the pregnancy, you will need to get a note from your doctor or midwife.

Am I entitled to any financial help?

Help with childcare

Funding up to the value of £160 per week is available, up to age 20, to enable young parents to continue their education at school and if they go on to college. Contact a Reintegration Officer for details or apply online:

⇨ Care to Learn: childcare while you learn – DirectGov (www.direct. gov.uk).

Educational Maintenance Allowance (EMA)

If you stay in education you may be entitled to claim up to £30 per week cash in your hands to help you carry on learning if you're 16, 17 or 18:

⇨ Education Maintenance Allowance – DirectGov (www.direct. gov.uk).

Benefits

Young parents can claim various sources of financial help, including child benefit when the child is born. For more help, visit the Citizens Advice Bureau website:

⇨ CAB – advice for parents aged under 16 (www.adviceguide.org.uk).

Who can I talk to for more advice?

The education department has a worker who will work with you, your parents and the school to make sure you get all the help you need to complete your education. These people are known as Pregnancy Reintegration Officers.

⇨ The above information is reprinted with kind permission from East Sussex County Council's young people's website, Connexions 360. Visit www.connexions360.org.uk for more information.

© East Sussex County Council

Teenage pregnancy facts

Information from fpa

fpa

talking sense about sex

This article covers Government policy and key statistics on teenage pregnancy in England, Wales, Scotland and Northern Ireland (United Kingdom/UK). Please note that the data for each country may not be strictly comparable due to differences in methods of data collection and analysis.

⇨ The UK has the highest teenage birth and abortion rates in Western Europe.

⇨ Rates of teenage births are seven times those in the Netherlands, double those in France and more than twice those in Germany.

⇨ While the teenage pregnancy rate in the USA is decreasing, the rate is nearly twice as high as in the UK – 72.2 per 1,000 15- to 19-year-olds in 2004.

⇨ Groups who are more vulnerable to becoming teenage parents include young people who are: in or leaving care; homeless; underachieving at school; children of teenage parents; members of some ethnic groups, involved in crime and living in areas with higher social deprivation.

⇨ Young women living in socially disadvantaged areas are less likely to opt for an abortion if they get pregnant.

England

⇨ Following a report from the Social Exclusion Unit in 1998, the Teenage Pregnancy Unit was set up and a ten-year strategy and action plan was implemented.

⇨ The target is to halve the under-18 conception rate by 2010 (from 46.6 per 1,000 in 1998) and to bring about a decline in the rate of conceptions to under-16s.

⇨ The aim is also to increase the participation of teenage parents in education, employment or training to reduce their long-term risk of social exclusion.

⇨ An Independent Advisory Group on Teenage Pregnancy was estab-lished in 2002 to provide advice to the Government and monitor overall success of the strategy.

⇨ Further guidance was published in 2006 to support more effective local implementation of the strategy.

⇨ Between 1998 and 2007 the teenage conception rate fell by 10.7 per cent in under-18s and by 6.4 per cent in under-16s.

Wales

⇨ As part of a general sexual health strategy, the Government aims to reduce teenage pregnancy rates and has developed an action plan to achieve this.

⇨ Between 2000 and 2005 the teenage conception rate fell by 9.8 per cent in under-18s and by 14.7 per cent in under-16s.

Scotland

⇨ The National Sexual Health Strategy for Scotland includes the target to reduce the under-16 conception rate by 20 per cent by 2010 (from 8.5 per 1,000 13- to 15-year-olds in 1995, to 6.8 per 1,000).

Northern Ireland

⇨ The Government aims to reduce the rate of births to teenage mothers under 17 years of age by 25 per cent by 2013 (from a baseline of 3.1 births per 1,000 females aged under 17 years in 2003–05).

⇨ Conception data is not available for Northern Ireland, due to the lack of complete data on the number of women having abortions. Abortion is only legal in exceptional circumstances and many women will travel to England to have an abortion.

⇨ In 2007, 235 women aged under 20 travelled to England to have an abortion, compared with 301 in 2000, although these numbers are likely to be an underestimate.

⇨ In 2007, there were 1,405 teenage births (under 20), a rate of 22.5 per 1,000 15- to 19-year-olds. The rate has fallen by 12 per cent since 2000.

July 2009

⇨ The above information is taken from the **fpa** factsheet *Teenage pregnancy* and is reprinted with permission. Visit www.**fpa**.org.uk for more information or to view references for this piece.

© *fpa*

Making a decision

Information from Education for Choice

If you are pregnant...

If you are pregnant, you have three basic choices:

⇨ CHOICE A: Continue the pregnancy and keep the baby.

⇨ CHOICE B: Continue the pregnancy and place the baby for adoption.

⇨ CHOICE C: End the pregnancy now by having an abortion.

If you are unsure of whether or not to continue with your pregnancy this article might help. It includes:

⇨ Questions that might help clarify your thoughts and feelings.

⇨ Places you can go to talk and get support with your decision.

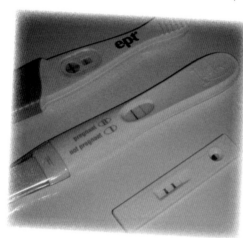

How do you feel about being pregnant?

Perhaps you planned to get pregnant because you wanted to have a baby, and that is still what you want most at this time. If so, you will probably decide on Choice A – continuing the pregnancy and keeping the baby.

If that is no longer what you want, or if you didn't intend to get pregnant in the first place, you can start by looking more closely at how you feel about being pregnant.

An unintended pregnancy can arouse many different feelings. In fact, most women find they have mixed or conflicting feelings.

For example, you might feel:

⇨ worried about being able to manage a baby;

Education For Choice

⇨ afraid you'll have to give up other things that are important to you;

⇨ concerned about how other people may react.

At the same time, you might also feel:

⇨ happy to learn that you can get pregnant;

⇨ pleased to have the opportunity to have a baby;

⇨ Excited by a new and unique event in your life.

It might help to list the different feelings you have right now about being pregnant. (When you can't think of any more, go on to the next section. Later, if you think of other feelings, you can add them to your list.)

What are your plans and dreams?

Here are some good questions to ask yourself about your life right now and about your future:

⇨ What are two or three things that matter most to me in my life right now?

⇨ What are two or three things that I hope to have or achieve in the next five or ten years?

In order to have or achieve those things:

⇨ How would having a baby help?

⇨ How would adoption help?

⇨ How would abortion help?

What would I lose or give up right now:

⇨ If I have the baby?

⇨ If I place the baby for adoption?

⇨ If I have an abortion?

How would other people react who matter to me (such as my partner, parents, friends)?

⇨ If I have the baby?

⇨ If I place the baby for adoption?

⇨ If I have an abortion?

What are your values? What do you believe?

Up to this point, you've been looking at the possible effects of different decisions on your plans and dreams. Now look at your thoughts, values, and beliefs about your situation and the different choices.

An unintended pregnancy can arouse many different feelings. In fact, most women find they have mixed or conflicting feelings

---

Following are some statements people often make. Check the ones that fit for you, and write in other thoughts you have.

CHOICE A: *Having a baby and keeping it*

⇨ I feel ready to take on the tasks of being a parent.

⇨ Some people have said they will help me.

⇨ I want a child more than I want anything else.

⇨ My partner and I both want to have a baby.

⇨ I think I am too young (or too old) to have a baby.

⇨ I don't believe I can manage to raise a child properly.

⇨ Having a child now would stop me from having the life I want for myself.

⇨ I feel ready to take on the tasks of being a parent.

CHOICE B: *Having a baby and putting it up for adoption*

⇨ I could continue the pregnancy and give birth, without having to raise the child.

⇨ I could help the child have parents who want it and can care for it.

⇨ I could postpone being a parent myself until later in my life when I feel ready.

⇨ I like the idea of giving someone else the baby they can't create themselves.

⇨ I don't think I could give up the baby after nine months of pregnancy and delivery.

⇨ I would not like living with the idea that someone else has my baby.

⇨ I would worry about whether the baby was being well treated. My family would rather have the baby stay in the family than go to strangers.

CHOICE C: *Having an abortion*

⇨ I would like to postpone being a parent until my situation is better (older, finished school, more financially secure, in a stable relationship).

⇨ I don't want to be a single parent.

⇨ My partner doesn't want a baby, and I want to consider his feelings.

⇨ An abortion is a safe and sensible way to take care of an unwanted pregnancy.

⇨ My religious beliefs are against abortion.

⇨ I would not like living with the idea that someone else has my baby.

⇨ I'm afraid I might not be able to get pregnant again.

⇨ My family (or someone else who is important to me) opposes abortion.

Mixed feelings?

If you – like so many women – have mixed feelings about being pregnant and about each of the choices open to you, making a decision can feel scary and difficult. In making your decision, it is helpful to know your feelings, to name them, and to look at them. To show how you are feeling right now, try to finish each of these sentences.

The idea of having a baby makes me feel_____because_____

The idea of placing a baby for adoption makes me feel_____ because_____

The idea of having an abortion makes me feel_____because_____

Now that you have explored your choices, obtained more information, and clarified your feelings and values about the choices, you may be ready to make a decision.

Since you probably have conflicting feelings about each choice, you may find that whatever decision you make won't feel like the 'perfect' decision. It is natural to continue to have some

mixed feelings. Ask yourself, 'Can I handle those feelings?' If your answer is 'Yes', you are ready to act on your decision.

No one can predict the future.

No one can be certain what all of the consequences of any choice may be. What you can do, however, is carefully consider your plans, your values and your feelings, and then make the best decision you can at the time.

If you cannot decide, you may need to get more information about your choices or talk with someone you trust – not to decide for you, but to help you decide what you think will be best for you. That person could be a:

⇨ parent or other family member;

⇨ close friend or partner who cares about you;

⇨ professional in a health service or young people's service.

Reprinted and adapted with permission from the National Abortion Federation, www.prochoice.org. Information taken from *Unsure About Your Pregnancy?* (copyright 1992)

⇨ The above information is reprinted with kind permission from Education for Choice. Visit www.efc.org.uk for more information.

© *Education for Choice*

The worst in Europe

Information from Chris Bryant, MP for the Rhondda

Attitudes towards marriage, contraception and abortion have changed across the centuries as science has advanced, religion has retreated and society has been transformed. The changes have been dramatic, affecting the most intimate aspects of family life. Childbirth and puerperal fever no longer kill thousands of mothers every year. Women and men get married later in life – and live longer.

They have babies later in life. They have fewer babies and more of them survive into adulthood. And changing economic patterns have led more parents more deliberately to plan the size of their family.

In addition, new forms of contraception (and most especially the

pill) have meant that sex without the fear of conception either within marriage or without is a reality. Other fears persist, not least thanks to HIV/AIDS and other Sexually Transmitted Infections. But sex without fear of

conception is the modern norm, not the exception.

Yet we have a very real problem of teenage pregnancy in Britain. The statistics give a stark picture, especially in deprived communities.

⇨ We have by a considerable way the highest rate of teenage pregnancies in Western Europe – five times that of Holland, three times that of France and double that of Germany – and the second highest rate in the world.

⇨ Most teenage pregnancies in England and Wales are to the poorest girls in the poorest parts of the country.

⇨ And many teenage mums were themselves the children of lone teenage mums.

It is a depressing story, not least in my own constituency, where we have the equivalent of 20 teenage pregnancies per secondary school every year.

The myths

There are, however, many myths around teenage pregnancy.

⇨ Many people believe that girls get pregnant so as to get a flat of their own from the Council. In fact 90% of teenage mums live in other people's homes – normally their parents'.

⇨ Many believe that the number of teenage pregnancies is rising. In fact the peak was between 1995 and 1997 and there has been a steady, though fairly small fall since 1997.

⇨ Many believe that British teenagers are just more promiscuous than their European counterparts, which is why we have higher levels of teenage pregnancy. In fact there is little evidence that we are any different in this regard from the rest of Europe.

⇨ The media often focus on the youngest teenage mums. In fact more than half of teenage pregnancies were to 18-year-olds and only 6% to under-16-year-olds.

⇨ Some have suggested that non-whites are more likely to become teenage mums. In fact 89% of teenage mums are white British and the lowest rates of teenage pregnancy are found amongst Asian women.

The facts

Statistics abound when it comes to teenage pregnancy. Figures tend to be calculated either by numbers of conception or live birth per 1,000 and are often separated by conceptions to girls under 20, under 18 and under 16. Confusingly, some figures are referred to as 'teenage' when they properly refer to under-18s. I shall use teenage to mean under 20.

⇨ Teenage pregnancy rates in the UK peaked between 1995 and 1998, but the UK still has the highest rate of teenage pregnancy in Europe.

⇨ There were 341 conceptions to girls under 14 in 2004 in England and Wales. 61.3% led to legal abortions. There were 7,613 conceptions to girls under 16, 42,150 to girls under 18 and 101,260 to girls under 20.

⇨ In 2005 there were 41.1 conceptions per 1,000 girls aged 15 to 17 in England, representing an overall decline of 11.8% since 1998 and the lowest level for 20 years.

Teenage pregnancy rates in the UK peaked between 1995 and 1998, but the UK still has the highest rate of teenage pregnancy in Europe

---

⇨ The figure for under-16 conceptions in England in 2005 was 7.8 per 1,000 girls aged 13 to 15. This is 12.1% lower than the 1998 rate of 8.8.

⇨ Half of all conceptions under 18 occur in the UK's 20% most deprived wards.

⇨ Rates have fallen in some areas, but in others they have risen. Lambeth fell marginally between 1998 and 2004, by 1.5%, but Barking and Dagenham rose by 32.6%, Blackpool by 11.6% and Torbay by 13.0%.

⇨ Figures have fallen similarly in Wales, but from 2002 to 2004 the rate in Torfaen rose from 47.8 to 66.9 per 1,000.

⇨ Just over a quarter (27%) of births to teenage mothers in England and Wales were registered solely by the mother.

⇨ Maternity rates vary across the UK. In 2004 in England and Wales there were 36 maternities per 1,000 females, in Scotland 21 and Northern Ireland 23.

⇨ The proportion of teenage mothers aged 16 to 19 in education, employment or training has increased from an average of 23.1% in 1997–99 to an average of 29.2% in 2004-06.

⇨ The UK Labour Force Survey suggests that between April and July 2007 the percentage of mothers aged 16 to 19 in employment was 20.7%, ILO unemployed was 8.5% and 70.8% were economically inactive (though this would include those in education).

Welsh facts

⇨ Wales continues to have a higher teenage pregnancy rate than England – with 43.6 conceptions per 1,000 girls in 2005, compared to 41.3 in England.

⇨ The figures for under-18 pregnancies in Wales were similar, but higher than in England. In 2005 there were 43.3 pregnancies under-18 per 1,000 (a fall of 9.8%), though many fewer led to abortions than in England (38.6% in Wales and 46.9% in England). In absolute terms there were 2,605 conceptions to girls under 18 in Wales in 2004, 434 under 16.

⇨ There were 457 conceptions in 2005 to Welsh girls aged under 16, up from 434 in 2004. Conception rates for girls aged under 16 decreased every year between 1999 and 2004 but increased slightly to 7.9 per 1,000 girls aged 13 to 15 in 2005.

⇨ In 2005 there were an estimated 2,521 conceptions to girls aged under 18, down from 2,605 in 2004. Conception rates for girls aged under 18 decreased from 45.1 per 1,000 girls aged 15 to 17 in 2004 to 43.6 in 2005.

⇨ In 2005 there were around 6,100 conceptions to females aged under 20, down from around 6,200 in 2004. The conception rate for females aged under 20 decreased from 64.2 per 1,000 females aged 15 to 19 in 2004 to 63.1 in 2005.

⇨ Figures by local authority area for conception rates under 18 show Wrexham with the highest rate in Wales at 62.7 per 1,000, up from 56 in 2003, followed by Torfaen (59.7), Caerphilly (53) and Rhondda Cynon Taff (52.7).

⇨ In Rhondda constituency, the figure for live births was 43.4 per 1,000 teenage girls. This compares to 28.9 in England and 33.7 in Wales.

But is teenage pregnancy a problem?

Above all, the statistics show that being a teenage mum is bad for you. You are less likely to be in good health or to complete your education and more likely to live in poor housing and spend long periods of your life on benefits. As one sixth-form girl put it to me at Treorchy Comprehensive School, 'There's a problem because girls won't finish their education because of the stresses of having a baby and they'll end up on benefit for ever.' And in the words of another, 'With benefits you're still poor.'

There are real dangers. In particular:

⇨ Babies of teenage mums tend to have a lower than average birth weight.

⇨ Infant mortality is 60% higher than for babies of older women.

⇨ Just 44% of mothers under 20 breastfeed, compared to 64% of 20- to 24-year-olds and up to 80% of older mothers.

⇨ Most depressingly, the daughters of teenage mothers are more likely to become teenage mums themselves.

Teenage pregnancy cannot be considered, of course, in isolation from other sexual health issues. Between 1991 and 2001, the number of new episodes of sexually transmitted infections (STIs) seen in Genitourinary Medicine (GUM) clinics in England, Wales and Northern Ireland doubled from 669,291 to 1,332,910. Young people, in particular females under the age of 20, bear the burden of sexually transmitted infections. Between 1997 and 2006 there was a 347% increase in the numbers of chlamydia infections in 16- to 19-year-old boys and 160% for girls.

Although some teenage mothers have immensely supportive families and cope with remarkable resilience, many find bringing up a baby very tough. When I visited the excellent Books and Babies project for pregnant schoolgirls and mothers under 16 in Nantgarw, many of the girls highlighted the real problems they had had: problems telling their parents they were pregnant, problems sorting housing and finances, problems with the dads, problems at school. One girl was just 13. Another had been thrown out by her mother

when she was only 14. Another was keen to move in with her 19-year-old boyfriend but was finding it impossible to get a flat unless she pretended she was going to live on her own. These are immensely tough issues for teenagers to cope with – and they showed remarkable cheerfulness.

One of the girls, Katie Wood, wrote, 'I find that I stress over any little thing most of the time and half of it is nothing to worry about but I can't help making a deal out of nothing. I can go a couple of months being fine, then I will have a week or so where things get on top of me and I just end up breaking down and crying about everything.'

Joy Starling, who runs Books and Babies, underlined to me the real emotional difficulties the girls face: 'Many of the girls suffer from acute depression and have real problems when their babies become toddlers. The children then end up being a problem because they've just not had enough support. The girls are desperate to come back to us, but we're only able to help until they are 16. Some girls will have a second baby when they're still teenagers because they remember the warm feeling of the early days.'

One final reason for worrying about the number of teenage pregnancies is of course the number of teenage abortions. In England in 2005 there were 18,628 under-18 abortions and in 2006 47% of pregnancies ended in abortions. 19-year-old girls are now the most likely age group to have an abortion.

⇨ The children of teenage mums have higher rates of infant mortality than children born to older mothers, are more likely to be born premature – which has serious implications for the baby's long-term health – and have higher rates of admissions to A&E. In the longer term, children of teenage mothers experience lower educational attainment and are at higher risk of economic inactivity as adults.

Babies of teenage mums tend to have a lower than average birth weight

---

⇨ The pressures of early parenthood result in teenage mothers experiencing high rates of poor emotional health and well-being – which impacts on their children's behaviour and achievement.

⇨ They often do not achieve the qualifications they need to progress into further education and, in some cases, have difficulties finding childcare and other support they need to participate in Education, Employment or Training (EET). Consequently, they struggle to compete in an increasingly high-skill labour market.

⇨ The above information is reprinted with kind permission from Chris Bryant MP. Visit www.teenagemums.org.uk for more information.

© Chris Bryant MP, 2008

It takes two to make a teenage pregnancy

The latest abortion statistics caused outrage – and, as usual, the right-wing media seem to think girls are to blame

The right-wing media should be celebrating the latest set of abortion figures that were released last week. After the years they've spent denouncing so-called feckless teenage mums, I almost expected to hear some kind of collective gasp of relief when the news was announced that not only have teenage pregnancies reduced in the last 12 months, but more teenage girls are opting to terminate their pregnancies.

> **If the alternative to 'children are aborting babies' is 'children are having babies' then I know which one I'm more comfortable with**

But no, 'credit where credit's due' has never been a mantra extolled by the likes of the *Daily Mail* or the *Telegraph*; so instead of headings along the lines of: 'Good grief, some teenagers are actually capable of acting responsibly,' or 'Forget ending benefits and reducing social housing; it looks like sex education is starting to work,' we got: 'Abortions for under-14 girls have soared by 21%' and 'Teenage abortions surge.'

If these headlines were all you read it would be easy to come away with the impression that hordes of promiscuous 12-year-olds are queuing up outside the nation's abortion clinics, setting off on the first steps of degenerate careers that will, no doubt, in the fevered imaginings of our self-appointed morality police at least, involve multiple terminations before they've even sat their first GCSEs.

By Cath Elliott

'Children are aborting babies,' cried Nadine Dorries, seemingly oblivious to the fact that her anti-choice crusade failed miserably in the House of Commons only a matter of weeks ago, and that the best thing she can do now is change the record and try to rescue some credibility as an MP before the next election comes round. But fortunately for the rest of us, those with our feet firmly on the ground and our bulls**t detectors switched on, there's media scaremongering, and then there's the figures themselves.

Yes, an increase from 135 to 163 under-14s having abortions amounts to a 21% rise (not 23% Nadine, at least try and get your facts straight); but 28 more abortions nationwide among younger girls is hardly an indication that the country's going to the dogs, or that chastity belts and forced temporary sterilisation should form part of the personal, social and health education curriculum.

Of course it would be better if no young girls were getting pregnant; I think I can safely say that's the one area where Dorries and I are probably in agreement. But if the alternative to 'children are aborting babies' is 'children are having babies' then I know which one I'm more comfortable with, and it's not the one that involves 12- and 13-year-old girls trying desperately to stop their babies crying so they can settle down and get on with their homework.

But then women's and girls' lives have never been a priority for those who fetishise the foetus; it's the potential life that's more important here, not the life that already exists. And that's why the headlines aren't more celebratory; because as far as the misogynistic moral crusaders are concerned, licentious Lolitas getting knocked up when they're barely out of nappies themselves aren't worth caring about anyway.

Besides which, if every teenage girl who found herself pregnant chose to abort, who on earth would the

Mail and the *Telegraph* have left to rail against? If there were no more teen pregnancies and underage single parents, who could they blame then for societal breakdown and juvenile delinquency? They need teenage mums so they can lay everything at their feet; get rid of them and the Tory press might be forced to concede that poverty and social exclusion have far more impact on people's lives than they've ever been prepared to admit. They might be forced to confront the elephant in the room, capitalism and unfettered greed; no, it's far easier to blame all the country's ills on promiscuous women. It's the same old same old, and teenage girls are once again in the firing line; they're damned if they do and damned if they don't.

The one thing that's been missing throughout this debate has been any mention of the involvement of men and boys in these pregnancies

---

Of course the one thing that's been missing throughout this debate has been any mention of the involvement of men and boys in these pregnancies. Now unless I've missed something, and I don't recall walking around with my eyes shut for the last few years, there hasn't been a sudden invasion of the heavenly host flying around and bringing tidings of great joy to all humankind: these girls didn't get pregnant by themselves. But you wouldn't know that to read the press. The focus as always is on the girls, who all appear to have woken up one morning and miraculously found themselves pregnant. So where's all the hand-wringing about the numbers of men and boys having sex with underage girls? Where's their responsibility in all this?

What's also missing is any kind of breakdown of these figures. How many of the pregnancies were the result of incest for example, or of rape? How many of the girls were coerced?

And how many were vulnerable young women with mental health issues or a background of physical and emotional abuse who thought consenting to sex would lead to the kind of loving relationship their lives had so far lacked?

Is it really too much to ask for some kind of analysis of statistics like this before they're published in future, before the headline writers and the scaremongerers go into their predictable hysterical overdrive? Chance would be a fine thing. After all, why look for an explanation when a soundbite will guarantee coverage? Why search for reasons when yet another opportunity presents itself

for even more woman-blaming and misogyny?

Girls eh? What are they like?

23 June 2008

© Guardian Newspapers Limited 2010

How many teens get pregnant?

Brook uncovers public ignorance over teenage pregnancy

Leading sexual health charity Brook has announced shocking figures revealing the extent of the general public's misunderstanding of the UK's teenage pregnancy rate. 95% of people over-estimate the rate of under-16s who get pregnant each year and the same amount are unaware of the significant drop in this figure over the last decade.

Brook commissioned Ipsos MORI to undertake a poll of 1,986 people to find out the public's perception of pregnancy rate amongst under-16s in England.

The poll found that 95% of people over-estimated the rate of under-16s getting pregnant each year. Just 5% were able to provide a close estimate of the teenage pregnancy rate, which is, in fact, less than 1%.

Young people themselves thought that the rate was particularly high – with 23% of 15- to 24-year-olds thinking that the rate of under-16s getting pregnant each year is over 40%, compared with 16% of people aged 25 or over.

Overall, 81% of respondents thought the rate had increased in the last 20 years, while it has actually decreased by 12.6% since 1998, the baseline for the Teenage Pregnancy Strategy.

Simon Blake, Brook's Chief Executive, said: 'With barely a week going by without a media story about teenage pregnancy, it's not surprising that the public believe it to be much more common than it actually is.

'This is particularly confusing for young people who may well think that teenage pregnancy is normal. It also fuels the myth that teenage pregnancy is escalating and nothing can be done. In fact significant reductions of many areas of the country shows that change is possible and we know what works to help young people prevent early pregnancy.'

30 September 2008

⇨ The above information is reprinted with kind permission from Brook. Visit www.brook.org.uk for more information.

© Brook

Parenthood?

Information from Education for Choice

What exactly is parenting?

Parenting is a lifelong commitment, and means being the legal guardian and carer of a child, usually one that you give birth to or adopt, though some people become parents to the children of their partner.

How do I find out about parenting?

There are lots of resources and organisations available to help and support parents, including younger parents. These include:
⇨ YWCA;
⇨ Parentline Plus;
⇨ Sure Start;
⇨ Maternity Alliance.

What do I need to be a good parent?

Parenting is a big responsibility. As well as very practical needs such as money, somewhere to live, clothing and equipment, you will also need support from other people, love and patience. If you want to either work or continue your education you will need childcare arrangements in place.

Must the father of the baby be involved?

The decision about whether to continue with a pregnancy or not rests with the woman, though you may want to involve your partner in the decision-making.

If you decide to continue the pregnancy and become a parent, you may wish your partner to have a role. This may be something he is willing and happy to do. Having the practical and emotional support of the father may be very helpful in the long run.

If he does not want to be involved, he may still be compelled to make a financial contribution to the child.

What happens after the baby is born?

After the birth, you may stay in hospital overnight, or longer, depending on how the birth went and the health of you and your baby. You will need to register the birth within 42 days – the hospital staff will give you guidance on this, or you can call the General Register Office, 0151 471 4805.

Once you are back at home, you will get regular visits from a health visitor or midwife, to see if you need any help and to monitor the baby's development.

What if I change my mind?

If you decide against becoming a parent, you may still have the option of ending the pregnancy, though this will depend on how advanced the pregnancy is. You will also have the option of putting the child up for adoption.

Can I keep it secret?

You might be tempted to keep the pregnancy secret while you pluck up the courage to talk to your parents or partner, but it is important to get good medical care and advice from early on in pregnancy. As soon as possible, talk to a professional who can help you and will keep your conversation confidential.

You might want to continue with the pregnancy against the wishes of your family or partner. If you feel that you are at risk of harm within the home because of your decision, you need to contact someone who can help:

Childline: tel 0800 1111
www.childline.org.uk
Connexions: tel 080 800 13 2 19
www.connexions-direct.com

Making the decision

The decision you make about your pregnancy is very important and finding out information on all of your options will be essential in making up your mind about it.

Ignoring your pregnancy, or leaving your decision to the last minute, however, could mean that your options are limited.

⇨ The above information is reprinted with kind permission from Education for Choice. Visit www.efc.org.uk for more information.

© *Education for Choice*

Young mums

Being a young mum can be daunting, especially if you're worried about money or how to look after yourself throughout your pregnancy. TheSite.org looks at some of the issues you may face

It's often presumed that if you're a young mum it was all a horrible accident, when in fact, many make the choice to start a family at a young age. At the same time, unexpected pregnancies aren't a problem unique to young mums - around 40% of women have unplanned pregnancies due to problems with contraceptives, or simply because they got carried away in the heat of the moment.

> **Unexpected pregnancies aren't a problem unique to young mums – around 40% of women have unplanned pregnancies**

If you're a young mum, you will no doubt share many of the same problems that older women face in pregnancy, but money, housing and health issues could be more of a concern.

Health and exercise

If you suspect you're pregnant it's best to get medical advice as soon as you can. Doctors and midwives aren't allowed to share personal information with anyone without your permission, whatever age you are.

'Even if the news of your pregnancy comes as a happy one, often one of the major causes of antenatal depression is the worry over where you're going to live with your new baby, how you're going to feed yourself, and how you can keep yourself healthy,' says midwife Cindy Hutchinson, who's working with Tommy's, the baby charity, on the project 'About Teenage Eating'.

If you're pregnant or have a child under the age of four, you're under 18, or you or your family are on benefits (Income Support, Jobseeker's

Allowance or Child Tax Credit), you may be eligible to sign up to the Government programme 'Healthy Start'. This will enable you to receive vouchers you can exchange for milk, fresh fruit and vegetables, infant formula and vitamin supplements.

Exercise will help you feel good about yourself and will enable your body to prepare for labour, birth and the demands of a newborn baby. Women's joints go through lots of change during pregnancy because the body produces the hormone relaxin. Because of this, your joints become looser and this means there's more risk of doing damage so it's important you avoid contact or high-impact sports. Instead, do gentle exercise like swimming, walking or yoga to minimise any jolts to your bump, and make sure you drink plenty of water.

Smoking

If you smoke during your pregnancy, your baby is more at risk of being born smaller or prematurely. This is because smoking raises the level of carbon monoxide in your bloodstream, which reduces the amount of oxygen available to your baby. It's also been shown that the impact of smoking on brain development and on the general health of your baby can last into childhood, and even later in life. 'The focus for helping young mums give up smoking should include helping them to sort out the stressful things in their lives that lead them to smoke in the first place,' says Cindy.

It's natural to feel guilty about something you may have done, or not done, in your pregnancy. 'Many of the unpleasant things that happen in pregnancy aren't necessarily related to things that women do, or don't do,' says Cindy. 'The best attitude for women who know they didn't have the healthiest lifestyle until they found out they were pregnant is to say that from now on they're going to do the best they can to be healthy.'

If you're worried you've done something to harm your unborn baby, speak to a professional who can talk you through your concerns and any possible problems. It may be

that you have no need to worry, or if there are potential issues, additional tests can be carried out to make sure everything is OK.

Housing and education

It doesn't matter what age you are when you get pregnant, you're still going to have the same responsibilities regarding motherhood. But if you're a young mum, this can be much harder. There may be pressures at school or college and decisions you have to make about your career. If you're under 20, you may be eligible for the Care to Learn Grant. This will help pay for childcare and extra costs.

Even if you've received positive responses from your partner and parents, you may have to move out simply to get a bigger place for you

and your baby to live. It isn't always easy to make ends meet on your own, so it's important you get the right information about benefits and housing entitlement.

Family support

Don't be scared to ask questions. Asking people for advice shows you're interested and want to make the best choices for you and your baby. 'Parents or family members should also see this curiosity as a positive thing,' says Cindy. 'If you explain your reasons for asking, they may be more likely to be supportive.'

It's hard for women of all ages to imagine what it's like to have a baby. Annie was 18 when she fell pregnant: 'My family were very surprised, but once they got over the initial shock

they were really supportive and listened to what I wanted to do, rather than telling me what to do.'

Often young people are faced with a barrage of criticism for getting pregnant from their family, friends, and even from the media. 'Strangers would look me up and down, especially when I got bigger, as I think they thought I looked too young to be a mum,' says Annie. 'All I could do was reassure myself that I knew I was strong enough to do it and it didn't matter what other people thought, my family's support was more important.'

⇨ The above information is reprinted with kind permission from TheSite. org. Visit www.thesite.org for more.
© TheSite.org

Young mums: the real story

Information from YWCA

The 'RESPECT young mums' campaign and the young mums' charter are based on an in-depth review, conducted by YWCA, of current research into the facts and figures surrounding young mums.

Combined with our unique experience of working with young mums, the research explodes common myths about teenage mothers.

Young mums: myths and facts

Myth: *'There is an epidemic of teenage pregnancy in the UK today.'*
Fact: Despite media headlines, overall teenage pregnancies have fallen nationally by 9.4% since 1999.
Myth: *'Young people are just too promiscuous.'*
Fact: In 2000, almost three-quarters of young women waited until they were 16 or over to have sex.
Myth: *'Young people today are careless about contraception.'*
Fact: In a recent study, only 7% of young men and 10% of young women aged 16 to 19 said they had used no form of contraception the first time they had sex. The proportion of young people not using any form

of contraception has decreased substantially in recent years.
Myth: *'In my day, girls were much less likely to get pregnant.'*
Fact: In 1970, young women aged 15 to 19 in England and Wales were almost twice as likely to become mums as they are today.
Myth: *'They only do it to get a council house.'*
Fact: Seven out of ten 15- and 16-year-old mothers and around half of 17- and 18-year-olds stay at home. In fact, most young mums have little knowledge of housing policy before getting pregnant – and what they do know often turns out to be wrong.
Myth: *'They only do it to get benefits.'*
Fact: Pregnant young women under 16 are not entitled to any benefits; 16- to 18-year-olds get between £33.50 and £44.05 a week. When their baby is born, they get between £102.01 and £112.56 per week. This has to pay for equipment like cots and prams, nappies and clothes, as well as food, bills, and any extra costs like childcare.

However, as with housing, most young mums have little knowledge

of social security policy before getting pregnant.
Myth: *'They can't look after their kids.'*
Fact: Evidence suggests that young parents take the responsibilities of parenthood very seriously: the needs of their children are always high on the agenda. Several studies show young mums cope just as well as older women in similar circumstances.
Myth: *'Young mums are all poor and have no education.'*
Fact: This one is a little closer to the truth. Young women from unskilled manual backgrounds are twice as likely to become teenage mothers as those from professional backgrounds. Young women with lower educational achievement – and low self-esteem – are also significantly more likely to become teenage mums. Unfortunately, this trend continues after young mums have their children.

⇨ The above information is reprinted with kind permission from YWCA. Visit www.ywca.org.uk for more information.
© YWCA

Justin's story

Information from Youngdads.co.uk

When my partner told me that she was pregnant, it was a shock to say the least! My heart began racing and I became extremely hot. There were so many questions darting through my mind; 'when? how long?' were the first I can remember. Instead of considering my partner's feelings, selfishness took over and I was solely interested in how it would affect me. To say I reacted badly is an understatement, but hearing the possibility of fatherhood made me so frightened. However scared I was, I should have realised that it must be so much worse for my partner.

As we were both young, she did not know straight away what she was going to do. I couldn't handle it. I needed to know. My impatience and inconsideration led to countless arguments and numerous sleepless nights. Deep down I felt I wasn't ready to be a father, but no one really ever

is. I knew I would be a great dad, but not knowing was eating me up inside! As the months passed, I felt ever closer to becoming a young father, but it seemed so surreal. When she told me of her decision, it still never actually sunk in until a few hours before my daughter was born. From the first contraction up until her birth, I was wriggling with excitement. I just could not wait to see the little person who had been living inside my partner for the past nine months. When I held my daughter in my arms for the first time, I felt a feeling that I had never felt before. I just never wanted to put her down. I could not believe that I had contributed to this brand new life.

My daughter is nearly eight months old now and I still have that feeling, every time I look into her eyes. I think this experience has taught me a lot about myself and changed my whole concept of life and difficult

situations. Looking back I know I could've handled the situation in a much more mature and adult manner and I would advise anybody in similar circumstances to put the other person's feelings before your own, and talk as much as possible to agree together and find civilised solutions.

⇨ The above information is reprinted with kind permission from Youngdads. co.uk. Visit www.youngdads.co.uk for more information.

© Youngdads.co.uk

Supervised homes for young mums

Confusion over Labour's plan to house young mothers in supervised homes

The prospect of supervised homes for teenage mothers was one of the most eye-catching policy announcements Gordon Brown made in his speech [at the 2009 Labour party conference], but the absence of any clear detail about how the commitment would be implemented triggered unease from charities who support young parents.

'I do think it's time to address a problem that for too long has gone unspoken, the number of children having children. For it cannot be right, for a girl of 16, to get pregnant, be given the keys to a council flat and be left on her own,' Brown told the conference.

'From now on all 16- and 17-year-

By Amelia Gentleman

old parents who get support from the taxpayer will be placed in a network of supervised homes. These shared homes will offer not just a roof over their heads, but a new start in life where they learn responsibility and how to raise their children properly. That's better for them, better for their babies and better for us all in the long run.'

Many such supervised homes exist already, but currently the decision of whether or not to be housed in one is left to the individual young parent. The Government's teenage pregnancy

strategy, launched in 1999, has already pledged to offer sheltered housing to those young parents unable to continue living at home. Despite this commitment, teenage parent support groups say sufficient resources have not so far been made available to fund enough buildings to be fitted out as mother-and-baby hostels – some areas have good provision, others have opened fewer homes.

The commitment to providing more of these homes was met with clear support from charities, but the suggestion lingering underneath that there might be an element of compulsion to the scheme elicited alarm.

No details of how the policy would work were immediately available from the Department for Children, Schools and Families, prompting one campaigner to ask if there was to be 'compulsory internment' of teenage mothers in hostels. There was no information available about whether there would be extra funding for such a scheme, or whether there would be any obligation for teenage parents to move into supervised housing.

The Teenage Pregnancy Independent Advisory Group welcomed the Prime Minister's announcement that there would be more support for young parents, adding: 'Many young parents are still living in unacceptable housing conditions and we welcome the Government's commitment to address this situation.'

However, in the absence of further details of the commitment, other charities were concerned by the tough tone that accompanied the pledge, which several saw as an attempt to engage with a middle-England contention that teenage girls get pregnant in order to get council accommodation.

Ann Furedi, chief executive of the British Pregnancy Advisory Service, said: 'This is an ill-thought-out sop to an ill-informed section of public opinion that misunderstands the causes and consequences of teenage pregnancy.'

Hilary Pannack, chief executive of Straight Talking Peer Education, a charity that works to reduce teenage pregnancies and to support teenage parents, said: 'There is an assumption in Gordon Brown's speech that all teenage parents are bad parents but this is not the case.'

In 1998, Labour announced a target of halving teenage pregnancy by 2010. Since then, overall rates of teenage pregnancy have fallen by 12.6% among under-18s and by 12.3% among under-16s.

29 September 2009

Supporting teenage mums

Teenage mothers need support, not 'discipline', says Ofra Koffman

Taking a tough stance on teenage mothers and assuring the public that they will not benefit from choosing to become parents is nothing new. When Gordon Brown promised last week that all parents aged 16 to 17 who get support from the taxpayer would be placed in a network of supervised homes, 'where they learn responsibility and how to raise their children properly', he raised a question that has haunted the debate on teenage parenthood: are teenage mothers delinquents who should be disciplined, or are they vulnerable children who should be protected?

If Brown is vowing to inculcate responsibility in a group of women through such 'supervision', he will not be the first to do so. This practice has a long history in relation to women who become pregnant out of wedlock.

Prior to the 'sexual revolution', it was unmarried mothers who were at the forefront of Government and public concern, studied by experts and managed by Government officers. They often lost their job or their home. Those without any alternative entered mother and baby homes managed by moral welfare associations, with religious affiliations, which believed that women who became pregnant out of wedlock were reckless individuals in need of 'rehabilitation'. Residents in the homes were subjected to a disciplinary regime aimed at transforming them into responsible, hard-working individuals.

In contrast with contemporary attitudes, moral welfare workers viewed positively a teenager's decision to raise her child, because the self-sacrifice of motherhood was seen as the antithesis of the selfish pursuit of sexual pleasure that led to the pregnancy. Yet there were also psychologists who claimed that unmarried mothers should have their children adopted.

By the late 1960s, societal tolerance of unwed mothers was growing, leading to a decline in the demand for a place in an institution. Some of the organisations managing the homes converted them into supervised accommodation for teenage mothers. The local authorities that supported the homes' previous work began funding this provision.

Special facilities for young mothers were described as stemming from a therapeutic need, rather than a disciplinary one. Psychologists argued that teenage mothers were not fully grown up psychologically and needed professional support and protection.

To this day, governmental rhetoric oscillates between claiming it seeks to protect 'child mothers' and promising society that it will discipline and deter them. Societal norms have radically changed since the days when women who engaged in extra-marital sex could find themselves confined in an institution. Yet the right of young women from disadvantaged backgrounds to become mothers is being delegitimised.

Contrary to the widespread belief that teenage mothers are motivated by financial incentives, research shows that many feel morally unable to terminate a pregnancy, and believe that by becoming mothers they are 'taking responsibility' for their actions. Penalising or institutionalising such women is not likely to reduce their numbers, but it will certainly create a climate in which reproductive rights are undermined. And if there is one thing that the liberalisation of sexual mores can teach us, it is that societal norms change, and when they do, the harsh treatment of marginal groups is remembered with shame.

⇨ Ofra Koffman is a visiting fellow at the Centre for the Study of Invention and Social Process, Goldsmiths, London University, and a member of the History & Policy network: historyandpolicy.org

7 October 2009

Condoms and contraception

Types of contraception: a quick guide

Contraception is the name for all the different methods of preventing pregnancy – all of which are very effective if used properly. Different methods suit people at different times in their lives. Visit a clinic to get more info and talk about what would suit you best.

Not having penetrative sex

There are many options regarding the kinds of sex people choose to have, and not being ready or choosing not to have vaginal sex means there is no risk of pregnancy.

Contraceptive injection (the 'jag')

Over 99% effective and lasts for 12 weeks. It releases the hormone progestogen slowly into the body. This stops ovulation, thickens the mucus to prevent sperm meeting an egg and thins the lining of the womb to prevent an egg implanting.

Implant

Over 99% effective and lasts for three years. It is a flexible tube put under the skin of the arm which releases the hormone progestogen (see the 'jag'). A local anaesthetic is used but no stitches are needed.

Intrauterine system (IUS)

Over 99% effective and works for five years. A small plastic device which releases the hormone progestogen when put into the womb.

Intrauterine device (IUD)

Around 99% effective and can work for three to ten years depending on the type. A small plastic and copper device is put into the womb.

Female and male sterilisation

Both are very effective, but involve a permanent decision about not having any or more children. The Fallopian tubes in women or the tubes carrying the sperm in men are cut or blocked to prevent sperm reaching an egg.

Contraceptive patch

Over 99% effective. A small patch (flesh coloured) is stuck on the skin (by yourself) once a week for three weeks, and then you have a break for one week before starting again. It contains the two hormones oestrogen and progestogen and works like the pill (see below).

Combined pill

Over 99% effective if taken regularly. It contains two hormones, oestrogen and progestogen, which stop ovulation, thicken cervical mucus to prevent sperm meeting an egg and thin the lining of the womb to prevent an egg implanting.

Contraceptive vaginal ring

Over 99% effective if used as directed. A flexible ring is inserted into the vagina (by yourself) and removed after three weeks. You have a break for a week before starting again. It contains the two hormones oestrogen and progestogen and works like the pill.

Progestogen-only pill

99% effective if taken properly. It contains the hormone progestogen, which thickens the cervical mucus to prevent sperm meeting an egg and thins the lining of the womb to prevent an egg implanting. Can be used by women who cannot take the combined pill with oestrogen. Your doctor or nurse will discuss this with you when they take a note of any personal or family illness.

Male condom

98% effective if used properly. Made of very thin latex (rubber) or polyurethane (plastic). It is a barrier method, and put on an erect penis it stops sperm from entering the female's vagina. It protects against pregnancy and most STIs.

Female condom

95% if used properly. It is made of soft polyurethane and again is a barrier method that stops the sperm entering the vagina. It fits inside the female vagina.

Diaphragm/cap

Between 92 and 96% effective. A flexible latex (rubber) 'cap' is put into the vagina to cover the cervix, which acts as a barrier to stop the sperm entering the womb. The first time it is fitted for you by a nurse or doctor, as there are different sizes. They teach you how to use it, and then you put it in yourself each time before you have sex.

Natural family planning

Probably up to 98% effective if followed precisely. The fertile and infertile times (when you are most likely to get pregnant) of your menstrual cycle are worked out. This shows the times in your cycle when you are less likely to get pregnant if you have sex. Some faith groups strongly support this method of contraception. Most people need to be taught how to do this by keeping charts of temperature and mucus changes in their body, which can be quite difficult.

Withdrawal

Not reliable. If a man withdraws his penis from the woman's vagina before he comes, there is still a risk of pregnancy as some 'pre-cum' is released before ejaculation.

⇨ The above information is reprinted with kind permission from Healthy Respect. Visit www.healthyrespect.co.uk for more information.
© Healthy Respect® is a registered trademark of the Lothian Health Board (2009)

Condoms: know the facts

There are a lot of myths about condoms so make sure you are aware of the facts before you have sex

MYTH It's safer if you use two condoms

TRUTH No it isn't, using two condoms at once is a really bad idea, whether it's two male condoms or a male and female condom. It increases the chances of them ripping so only use one at a time.

MYTH Condoms break easily

TRUTH No they don't. To avoid a condom breaking you need to put it on carefully, ensuring there is no air bubble at the end and be careful of sharp nails, jewellery or teeth. If one has been put on inside-out it'll be uncomfortable to roll on, so take it off and put a new one on. If one does break and you're not using any other contraception, go to a clinic, pharmacist or doctor as soon as possible and ask about emergency contraception. You will also need to go and be tested for sexually transmitted infections.

MYTH Condoms are the only type of contraception I need to think about

TRUTH No they're not. Condoms can provide protection from STIs and unintended pregnancy but to ensure the best protection it is recommended that you and your partner use a condom together with another form of contraception. There are many different types of contraception that can be used, including the implant, injection, coil or the pill, and it's worth exploring all the options.

MYTH You need extra lube. Vaseline is good

TRUTH No it's not. A bit of extra lubrication is good but don't use anything with oil in it as it can dissolve the condom – that includes baby oil, Vaseline and hand cream. Remember lipstick has oil in it too. Use a water-based lubricant such as KY jelly, Durex Play, Clinigel or Sensel from a pharmacy.

MYTH Condoms make him less sensitive

TRUTH Using a condom doesn't have to spoil the moment: they can make some men last longer before they come, which is good news for both of you. There are many different sizes, shapes, colours, textures and flavours of condoms, so enjoy finding the one that suits you both best.

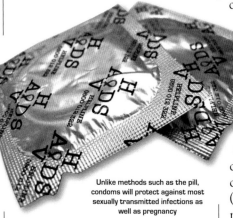

Unlike methods such as the pill, condoms will protect against most sexually transmitted infections as well as pregnancy

MYTH Condoms cut off his circulation

TRUTH No they don't. A condom can stretch to 18 inches round. He'll be fine. Again, remember there are many different shapes and sizes available to try.

You can buy condoms at any age. You can get them free, at any age, from community contraception clinics, Brook centres and NHS sexual health clinics.

MYTH I'm on the pill, so we don't need condoms

TRUTH Yes you do. The pill does not protect you or your partner from STIs. Plus, if you've forgotten to take a pill, been sick or are using antibiotics, the effectiveness of the pill is reduced and you could still get pregnant.

MYTH If I ask to use a condom, my partner will think less of me

TRUTH Insisting that you use a condom suggests that you know how to take care of yourself and shows that you know what you want, which can be very sexy.

MYTH You don't need a condom if you're having oral sex

TRUTH Yes you do, you should use a condom for oral sex because gonorrhoea, chlamydia and herpes can be passed to each other this way.

MYTH You have to be 18 to buy condoms

TRUTH No you don't, you can buy condoms at any age. You can also get them free, as well as getting confidential advice, at any age from community contraception clinics (formerly family planning clinics), Brook centres, Sexual Health (GUM) clinics, FE colleges and young people's clinics.

MYTH I don't need a condom – I only sleep with nice people

TRUTH STIs don't know or care if you're nice or not. The way someone looks is no indicator of whether they have an STI. Many STIs don't show any symptoms so you could infect each other without even knowing it.

MYTH If it's a condom, it's safe

TRUTH Not necessarily – novelty condoms aren't safe. Always choose condoms that carry the European CE or Kitemark, which is a recognised safety standard. Also check the date on the packet as condoms don't last forever.

22 September 2008

⇨ The above information is reprinted with kind permission from NHS Choices. Visit www.nhs.uk for more information on this and other related issues.

© *Crown copyright*

Should the pill be available without prescription? Yes

Two areas in London are piloting over-the-counter oral contraceptives. Daniel Grossman argues that the policy should be widely adopted but Sarah Jarvis believes it is the wrong approach to reducing unplanned pregnancy

Oral contraceptives are the most widely used hormonal method of contraception globally and the most commonly used reversible method in less developed countries other than China. The pill is highly effective and with perfect use has a failure rate of only 0.3% in the first year. But in practice, failure is much higher – closer to 8% or 9%. In most countries, women must have a doctor's prescription to obtain oral contraceptives, although many developing countries do not enforce this and pills are effectively available over the counter.

Data from the United States suggest that, for at least some women, the prescription requirement represents a barrier to both initiation and continuation of hormonal contraceptives. A US national survey of women in 2004 reported that 41% of women not currently using contraception said they would start using the pill, patch or vaginal ring if it were available directly in a pharmacy. Another study found that travel away from home and running out of pill packs were frequent reasons women missed pills, a common cause of

By Daniel Grossman, senior associate, assistant clinical professor

contraceptive failure. Participants in a Scottish study of attitudes to contraception also commented that getting an appointment with a general practitioner can be hard.

Safety

Is it safe for women to access oral contraceptives without a prescription? Over 50 years of experience have shown oral contraceptives to be very safe. In every age group, the risk of cardiovascular death among healthy non-smokers who take the pill is lower than the same risk for women carrying a pregnancy to term.

However, the question remains whether women need to visit a clinician to determine whether oral contraception is appropriate for them. Ideally, doctors or nurses screen women for contraindications to the pill using evidence-based criteria, such as those of the World Health Organization. But in practice this screening does not always take place.

Research from Mexico, where the pill is widely available without a prescription, found that women obtaining the pill without visiting a clinician were no more likely to have contraindications to its use than women who saw a doctor. Two US studies found that women were able to identify if they had contraindications to oral contraceptives using a checklist, although older women were more likely to have unrecognised hypertension. These data are not surprising, given that, other than hypertension, all of the contraindications are based on history and require little clinical judgment.

The pill is highly effective and with perfect use has a failure rate of only 0.3% in the first year

Another concern about making oral contraceptives available without a prescription is women will not use them correctly. Again, few data suggest that clinician counselling is useful, and even when a clinic visit is required, compliance is not perfect. Oral contraceptives are available over the counter in Kuwait, and a study there found that compliance and continuation were no different between women who consulted a doctor and those who did not. A recent analysis of data from California found that women given 13 pill packs when they first started continued the method significantly longer and experienced fewer gaps in use than women given only one or three packs, suggesting that freer access improves continuation. Pharmacist provision of

NO! You can't have it unless we say so!

hormonal contraception was recently shown to be feasible and acceptable to women in Washington state.

Access to care

Would women miss out on other preventive services, such as cervical smear tests or screening for sexually transmitted infections, if they were not required to visit a clinician? Neither of these screening tests is medically required before prescribing oral contraceptives, and there has been a growing movement to unbundle these services in the US. The national survey mentioned above found that among women not currently using contraception, 88% had had a smear test in the previous 24 months. In fact, given the recent definitive evidence that oral contraceptive use reduces the risk of ovarian cancer, it has been argued

that the prescription requirement unnecessarily limits access to this effective chemoprophylactic agent.

Although there are concerns in the US about the costs to women of obtaining oral contraceptives over the counter, in some states there is a precedent for maintaining government funding for over-the-counter emergency contraception for women on low incomes.

Making oral contraceptives available without a prescription would not eliminate the option of clinician consultation. Indeed, research in Mexico indicates that women move between provision sources, and more than half of women who obtain their pills from a pharmacy began use under a physician's care. Women who value a clinician's input or have questions about their risk profile would still be able to consult with a physician or

nurse – but they would not be required to. The prescription requirement is an out of date, paternalistic barrier to contraceptive use that is not evidence-based. If governments are committed to addressing the challenge of unintended pregnancy – and the related problem of maternal mortality in the developing world – health systems must create mechanisms to allow freer access to hormonal contraception for all women at low or no cost.

Cite this as: BMJ 2008; 337:a3044
Competing interests: None declared
23 December 2008

⇨ The above information is reprinted with kind permission from BMJ Publishing Group. Visit www.bmj.com for more information or to view references for this article.

© BMJ Publishing Group

Should the pill be available without prescription? No

Two areas in London are piloting over-the-counter oral contraceptives. Daniel Grossman argues that the policy should be widely adopted but Sarah Jarvis believes it is the wrong approach to reducing unwanted pregnancy

The United Kingdom is top of a league in western Europe – and a very undesirable first place it is, too. The league table is that for teenage pregnancies, with rates of teenage motherhood in the UK, at 15%, around twice those of Germany (8%), three times those of France (6%), and almost four times those of Sweden (4%).

The implementation of a national teenage pregnancy strategy in 1999 has gone some way to reversing the rising trend of teenage pregnancies, but only by about 2% a year in the first five years after it was implemented. As with other lifestyle diseases such as diabetes, however, the UK still ranks far behind the United States, where 22% of women have a child before the age of 20.

Nevertheless, action still needs to be taken to address the underlying causes. The Department of Health

By Sarah Jarvis, women's health spokesperson

Social Exclusion Unit has highlighted complex reasons for the high rates of teenage pregnancy in the UK, including lack of education and mixed messages in the media. Societal

attitudes, Government housing policy for teenage mothers and media messages are largely beyond the remit of primary care's influence. Education about contraception, however, is not. And it is contraceptive use, rather than sexual activity, which correlates most closely with rates of unplanned pregnancy.

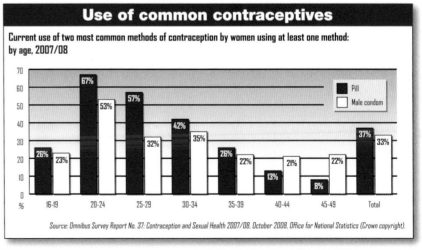

Use of common contraceptives

Current use of two most common methods of contraception by women using at least one method: by age, 2007/08

Source: Omnibus Survey Report No. 37: Contraception and Sexual Health 2007/08. October 2008. Office for National Statistics (Crown copyright).

Wrong method

In 2005, the National Institute for Health and Clinical Excellence (NICE) guidance highlighted low use of long-acting reversible contraception (intrauterine contraceptive devices, intrauterine system, progestogen-only subdermal implants and progestogen-only injectable contraceptives) compared with user-dependent methods such as the contraceptive pill as one of the reasons for high rates of unwanted pregnancy. This claim certainly fits with the evidence – about 8% of women of childbearing age in the UK (with a 15% teenage motherhood rate) use long-acting contraceptives compared with about 20% in Sweden, where the rate of teenage motherhood is 4%.

Although making the combined oral contraceptive pill available without prescription may be safe, it would not help. Those using the service would not, as the NICE guidance recommends, be offered a full range of contraception on every occasion. Oral contraceptives require daily compliance on the part of the patient, whereas all long-acting contraceptives are effective for at least three months, are at least as cost effective at one year as the oral contraceptives, and have similar satisfaction rates.

The major difference between long-acting and oral contraceptives is their reliability in practice. Compliance is low with oral contraceptives. In one study of women using oral contraception, 47% missed one or more pills per cycle, and 22% missed two or more. These women have almost a threefold increase in unintended pregnancy compared with women who take the pill consistently, and teenagers are the group with the highest non-compliance.

Long-acting contraceptives such as the intrauterine contraceptive device, intrauterine system and the progesterone-only subdermal implant, are effective for at least three years. Even the progestogen-only injectable contraceptive (depot contraception), which requires attendance for repeat injection every three months, is significantly more reliable than oral contraceptives. In a US study of teenagers offered

contraception after termination, repeat pregnancy rate was 29.7% for girls given the oral contraceptive compared with 14.2% for those given depot contraception.

Availability

Access to primary care services is less of a problem in the UK than in some other countries, particularly the United States. Over 99% of the UK population is registered with a general practitioner, and 85% of the population see a general practitioner at least once a year. Although 16- to 19-year-olds are more likely than other groups to use family planning clinics (rather than general practitioners) for contraception, 72% of teenagers still express a preference for attending the general practitioner for contraceptive services.

Oral contraceptives require daily compliance on the part of the patient, whereas all long-acting contraceptives are effective for at least three months

---

There is great untapped opportunity for general practitioners to encourage young women to use long-acting contraceptives – an analysis of the general practice records of 13- to 19-year-olds who had had a

termination showed that half had sought contraceptive advice from the general practitioner in the previous year and that 40% of these had been prescribed oral contraception. In addition, compared with matched controls, girls who had become pregnant were significantly more likely to have requested emergency contraception. This does not include the many chances for opportunistic discussion during attendances for other reasons.

The availability of emergency contraception without prescription has done little to change the rate of teenage pregnancies. This is hardly surprising, when among under-25s, only 37% use emergency contraception on every occasion that they have unprotected intercourse. Increased uptake of reliable, non user-dependent methods has to be the key. Rather than making a potentially unreliable method of contraception more easily available, our best avenue for reducing unplanned pregnancies is to encourage general practitioners to help their patients to make the best choices.

Cite this as: BMJ 2008; 337:a3056
Competing interests: SJ has been paid by Bayer for speaking at symposiums and writing educational articles.
23 December 2008

⇨ The above information is reprinted with kind permission from BMJ Publishing Group. Visit www.bmj.com for more information or to view references for this article.

Contraception and teenage pregnancy

Information from the Department of Health

2007 abortion data were published by the Department of Health on 19 June 2008 and show increases in the abortion rate for all women aged under 20, most markedly for those aged under 18. These data highlight that many PCTs need to significantly improve performance for the Public Service Agreement target to reduce under-18 conceptions by 50% by 2010 to be delivered. Reducing teenage conceptions is a Tier 2 Vital Signs indicator (national priority for local action). Between the 1998 baseline year and 2006 (the latest year for which data are available), the under-18 conception rate has fallen by 12.9%, and the under-16 rate has fallen by 12.6% over the same period. Within the overall reduction in all under-18 conceptions, the rate of births has fallen by 23%, while the rate of abortions has stayed stable. While teenage pregnancy rates are at their lowest rates for over 20 years, most areas are not on trajectory to meet their planned contributions to the PSA target.

The Teenage Pregnancy Strategy is multi-faceted and is based on the best international evidence on what works. One of the priority actions identified in the strategy is to ensure equitable access to the full range of contraception methods and provision of high-quality advice and support. There is increasing evidence that contraception can have a significant impact on teenage conceptions:

⇨ Around 80% of under-18 conceptions are in 16- and 17-year-olds, which is the age most young people become sexually active. It is therefore very important that they have access to effective contraception to prevent pregnancy.

⇨ Research published in the *American Journal of Public Health* in 2006 found that 86% of the decline in US teenage pregnancy rates between 1995 and 2002 could be attributed to improved contraceptive use.

⇨ DH and DCSF have produced joint Next Steps guidance to Primary Care Trusts and Local Authorities on accelerating delivery of the teenage pregnancy strategy. This highlights that provision of young people focused contraception/ sexual health services, trusted by teenagers and well known by professionals working with them, was the factor most commonly cited as having the biggest impact on conception rate reductions in high-performing areas.

Some methods of contraception are more effective at preventing pregnancy than others. The effectiveness of oral contraceptive pills depends on their correct and consistent use. A NICE guideline was published in 2005 which highlights that if 7% of women switched from the contraceptive pill to Long Acting Reversible Contraceptive [LARC] methods (defined as the intrauterine device [IUD], hormonal injection, intrauterine system [IUS] and contraceptive implant), the NHS could save around £100 million through reducing unintended pregnancies by 73,000 per annum.

In February 2008, the Public Health Minister, Dawn Primarolo, announced £26.8m new funding for 2008/09 from the Comprehensive Spending Review to improve access to contraception. The money for 2008/09 was invested as follows:

⇨ £12.8 million was included in Primary Care Trusts, main allocations.

⇨ The remaining £14 million was allocated by the Department of Health (£10m by the Sexual Health team and £3.5m by the Children and Young People's team to develop services in FE colleges), working with SHAs. Priorities for funding included teenage pregnancy 'hotspot areas' with high and increasing rates of conceptions and areas with high abortion and repeat abortion rates. The funding is being used to ensure equitable access to LARC methods, training and workforce and improving access to contraception following abortion.

⇨ £500,000k was invested nationally to develop a campaign, working with the Teenage Pregnancy Unit in the Department for Children, Schools and Families to highlight contraceptive choices available to women.

Further funding will be available in 2009/10 and 2010/11.

More detailed Good Practice Guidance for commissioning, contraception and abortion services is currently being finalised and will be published later this year.

5 February 2009

⇨ The above information is reprinted with kind permission from the Department of Health. Visit www. dh.gov.uk for more information.

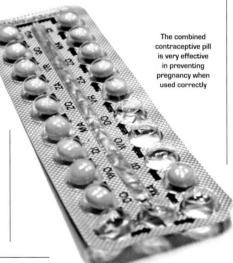

The combined contraceptive pill is very effective in preventing pregnancy when used correctly

More cash for contraception

Information from the Department for Children, Schools and Families

⇨ *£20.5m package to promote contraception.*
⇨ *Call for action to areas with high teenage pregnancy rates.*

An extra £20.5 million will help young people get better access to contraception and support for teenagers and raise the awareness of the risks of unprotected sex, Public Health Minister Dawn Primarolo and Young People's Minister Beverley Hughes announced today.

The cash supports the teenage pregnancy strategy that is focused on encouraging young people to delay early sex and to practise safe sex as and when they do become sexually active.

The new package of support and investment to promote the use of contraception includes:

⇨ £7 million for a new 'contraceptive choices' media campaign to raise awareness of the different options – including Long Acting Reversible Contraceptives (LARCs) – available to young people to prevent teenage conceptions;

⇨ £10 million for local health services to ensure contraception is available in the right places at the right time;

⇨ £1 million to support further education colleges develop and expand on-site contraception and sexual health services to help address the fact that 80 per cent of under-18 conceptions are among 16- to 17-year-olds.

⇨ A further £2.5 million will help develop a Healthy College programme and help all services meet the Department of Health 'You're Welcome' standards for young people friendly services.

Figures released by the Office of National Statistics today show that the increase in teenage pregnancy rates in the first three quarters of 2007 is due to a rise in unplanned conceptions ending in abortion, and not an increase in teenage mothers giving birth. However, the under-18 conception rate for the final quarter of 2007 is two per cent lower than the same quarter in 2006 – suggesting that the drive to reduce teenage conceptions is continuing in the right direction.

Where there have been rises, and given these have resulted in abortions not births, this suggests that young people are not accessing effective contraception and may be engaging in more risky behaviour – pointing to the need for better advice and information about sex and relationships both from their parents and in schools.

Young people say they would prefer advice from parents and that's why the Government has invested in support for parents to help them talk more openly to their children. The Government has already announced its intention to make Sex and Relationship Education (SRE) compulsory as part of Personal, Social and Health Education (PSHE), and all schools will be provided with new SRE guidance this September.

Evidence shows that where the Government's teenage pregnancy strategy is implemented rigorously, significant reductions in teenage pregnancy rates have been achieved, such as in Oldham where rates have dropped by 29 per cent. The Government wants this success replicated across the country and is today calling on all local areas to redouble their efforts to drive a robust approach to reducing teenage pregnancy rates.

Despite the rise in national figures in the last year, the long-term trend is still downward and overall there has been a 10.7 per cent reduction in under-18 conceptions and a 23.3 per cent decline in teenage births since the start of the Government's strategy in 1998. In 2006 the rates dropped to their lowest level in 20 years. Tackling teenage pregnancy requires sustained action by local authorities, the NHS, parents, schools, and young people themselves.

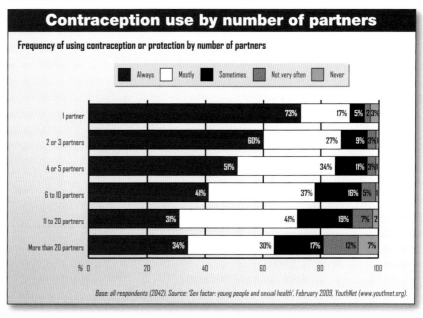

Contraception use by number of partners

Frequency of using contraception or protection by number of partners

Legend: Always | Mostly | Sometimes | Not very often | Never

Number of partners	Always	Mostly	Sometimes	Not very often	Never
1 partner	73%	17%	5%	2%	3%
2 or 3 partners	60%	27%	9%	3%	
4 or 5 partners	51%	34%	11%	3%	
6 to 10 partners	41%	37%	16%	5%	
11 to 20 partners	31%	41%	19%	7%	2%
More than 20 partners	34%	30%	17%	12%	7%

Base: all respondents (2042). Source: 'Sex factor: young people and sexual health', February 2009, YouthNet (www.youthnet.org).

Children and Young People's Minister Beverley Hughes said:

'Today's teenage pregnancy statistics are disappointing, although the reduction in the last quarter of 2007 over 2006 gives me cautious optimism that the drive to reduce teenage pregnancy/conceptions is still on track. There is no doubt that rates have come down where local areas have implemented the strategy properly, even in deprived areas.

'Young people need good advice and easy access to contraception when they become sexually active'

'The evidence suggests that more teenagers may have been engaging in risky behaviour and not using contraception, resulting in an increase in conceptions leading to abortion. Our strategy is to encourage teenagers to delay early sexual activity, but to use contraception when they do become sexually active.

'We have already announced our intention to make sex and relationship education (SRE) compulsory and we will be providing new SRE guidance to schools this September. This is in addition to more support for parents to help them talk more openly to their children about sex and relationships. And for the minority of families where parents are failing in their responsibilities we will continue our programmes of intensive family support which we know works in getting parents to do better by their children.

'Reducing teenage pregnancy requires everyone to play their part – parents, health and local authorities, and schools. Where progress has slowed, efforts must be redoubled and we will be focusing our challenge on those areas with high and increasing rates.'

Health Minister Dawn Primarolo said:

'Young people need good advice and easy access to contraception when they become sexually active. To help, we are improving access to contraception by providing an extra £20.5 million funding this year.

'We are supporting the NHS to offer women of all ages the full range of contraceptive choices, including long-acting reversible methods such as implants and injections which are virtually 100 per cent effective. And we're giving local health services more money to come up with innovative ways of making sure young women use their contraceptives properly, such as text message reminders.'

Further Education Minister Sion Simon said:

'The Further Education sector has an important contribution to make in tackling sexual health issues. Colleges are ideally placed to offer support and advice to young people, and this extra investment will allow them to develop and expand on-site contraception and sexual health services.

'Providing health advice services on-site avoids FE students having to take time off from their studies, helps them to deal quickly with health concerns that might be impacting negatively on their learning and can help avoid them dropping out of learning altogether.'

The Government has issued clear guidance on effective strategies which all areas must follow with a concerted and consistent approach. Ministers will be meeting with senior officials from Local Authorities and Primary Care Trusts in areas with high rates as well as receiving six monthly reports on the actions they are taking to strengthen their strategies. The Government has also taken action since 2007 to strengthen delivery of the strategy, which is not reflected in the statistics out today.

For the minority of families needing additional support, we have a range of parenting programmes designed to identify problems early and provide intensive help. These include the Family Nurse Partnerships for young mothers and Family Intervention Projects being expanded to all areas this year. From April this year, all areas will have at least two parenting experts to work with families and children experiencing serious problems.

In their guidance on Long Acting Reversible Contraceptives (LARC), NICE estimated that if seven per cent of women switched from the pill to LARC methods (doubling current usage to 15 per cent) the NHS could save around £100 million each year through reducing unplanned pregnancies by 73,000.

26 February 2009

⇨ The above information is reprinted with kind permission from the Department for Children, Schools and Families. Visit www.dcsf.gov.uk for more information.

© Crown copyright

About the Teenage Pregnancy Strategy

Information from the Department for Children, Schools and Families

The Government's Teenage Pregnancy Strategy represents the first coordinated attempt to tackle both the causes and the consequences of teenage pregnancy. The strategy's targets are:

⇨ Halve the under-18 conception rate by 2010, and establish a firm downward trend in the under-16 rate.

⇨ Increase the proportion of teenage parents in education, training or employment to 60% by 2010, to reduce their risk of long-term social exclusion.

All local areas have a ten-year strategy in place, with local under-18 conception rate reduction targets of between 40 and 60%. These local targets underpin the national 50% reduction target.

Key factors for reducing teenage pregnancy

Evidence from areas with the largest reductions has identified a range of factors that need to be in place to successfully reduce teenage pregnancy rates. All areas are now being asked to implement these factors, which are:

Engagement of delivery partners
Active engagement of all of the key mainstream delivery partners who have a role in reducing teenage pregnancies: health, education, social services, youth support services and the voluntary sector.

Selection of a senior champion
A strong senior champion who is responsible for the local strategy and can take the lead in implementing it.

Effective sexual health advice service
The availability of a well-publicised contraceptive and sexual health advice service which is centred on young people. The service needs to have a strong remit to undertake health promotion work, as well as delivering reactive services.

Prioritisation of sex and relationships education
High priority given to PSHE in schools, with support from the local authority to develop comprehensive programmes of sex and relationships education (SRE) in all schools.

Focus on targeted interventions
A strong focus on targeted interventions with young people at greatest risk of teenage pregnancy, in particular with looked-after children.

Are young people receiving reliable sexual health advice or relying on hearsay?

Training on SRE for partner organisations
The availability and consistent take-up of SRE training for professionals in partner organisations who work with the most vulnerable young people, such as Connexions personal advisers, youth workers and social workers.

Well-resourced youth service
Providing things to do and places to go for young people, with a clear focus on addressing key social issues affecting young people, such as sexual health and substance misuse.

Local delivery is supported by two national media campaigns: 'RU Thinking' and 'Want Respect? Use a Condom'. 'RU Thinking' is aimed at younger teenagers, promoting messages on delaying first sex and avoiding peer pressure. 'Want Respect? Use a Condom' is aimed at sexually active young people. It promotes condom use by associating the use of condoms with behaviour that will earn young people respect from their peers.

We also provide support for parents to talk to their children about sex and relationship issues, through the Time to Talk initiative delivered by Parentline Plus.

Improving outcomes

The strategy also includes action to improve outcomes for teenage parents and their children. The range of poorer outcomes they experience in comparison to older mothers includes:

Poor child health outcomes
Children born to teenage mothers have 60% higher rates of infant mortality and are at increased risk of low birth-weight which impacts on the child's long-term health.

Poor emotional health and well-being experienced by teenage mothers
Teenage mothers are three times more likely to suffer from post-natal depression and experience poor mental health for up to three years after the birth.

Teenage parents' poor economic well-being
Teenage parents and their children are at increased risk of living in poverty.

Teenage Parents Next Steps, published in July 2007, sets out what action local areas need to take to drive improvements in outcomes for teenage parents and their children.

⇨ The above information is reprinted with kind permission from the Department for Children, Schools and Families. Visit www.dcsf.gov.uk for more information.

© Crown copyright

The big question

Why is the teenage pregnancy rate so high, and what can be done about it?

Why are we asking this now?

The case of Alfie Patten, said to have fathered a child at the age of 13 with a girl of 15, has reignited controversies over sex and morality education, with Conservative party leader David Cameron believing the case is evidence that his claim that Britain has become a 'broken' society is right.

The case comes on top of the fact that statistics show that the UK has the highest percentage of teenage pregnancies in Western Europe – and is second only to the United States, according to figures compiled by the World Health Organization.

What is the Government's policy on sex education in schools?

A Government review of how the subject is broached in schools recommends that sex education should be a compulsory part of the national curriculum in primary and secondary schools under a new curriculum to be introduced in September 2010. However, the plan has provoked controversy – particularly among faith-based groups. As a result, a new review led by a respected East London headteacher, Sir Alasdair MacDonald, will look at the question of whether there should be an opt-out clause for parents who do not want their children to take part in the lessons.

Why was this review necessary?

Because statistics – in the form of our teenage pregnancy rates – make it obvious that we have not been successful in delivering this in the past. Currently secondary schools only have to teach the mechanics of sex in biology classes and not in conjunction with relationships and sexual health. Most schools do teach personal, social and health education (PSHE), but it is not compulsory.

A recent survey of pupils showed that four in every ten had received no sex education at school. Teaching of sex education in the UK also poses

By Richard Garner

particular problems in faith schools. For instance, contraception, abortion and homosexuality are against the teachings of the Catholic faith and there has been some controversy within Catholic schools where diocese have issued edicts barring their schools from allowing pro-choice groups into schools to talk about abortion.

The Government, said Mr Knight, is planning supplementary guidance for faith schools indicating that they must teach all elements of the curriculum alongside Catholic values.

> The teenage pregnancy rate in Holland is only one-fifth as high as that of the UK – only five births per 1,000 teenagers compared to the UK's 27

Why do we have the highest teenage pregnancy rate in western Europe?

Some would back David Cameron's 'broken Britain' line – arguing that there has been a general reduction of family values with less emphasis on marriage and a growth in single-parent families. Others would argue that today's youngsters have been subjected to 'sexploitation' – both by the commercial world as witnessed in several reports, most notably the recent inquiry into childhood by the Children's Society, which talked of advertisers aiming sexy clothing ads at an increasingly younger age group, and through the Internet with a report last week claiming that 'tens of thousands' of school and university websites worldwide had become affected by hardcore pornography. Dr

Tanya Byron, the TV psychologist who conducted a review of Internet use and video games for the Government, recommended that all schools should use an accredited service for their Internet provision – which can have blocks put on it to bar hardcore porn from websites used by pupils.

How is the issue tackled in countries with lower teenage pregnancy rates?

The teenage pregnancy rate in Holland is only one-fifth as high as that of the UK – only five births per 1,000 teenagers compared to the UK's 27. Its abortion rate per teenage head of the population is also one of the lowest in Europe. The approach to sex education, though, in a country where pupils are as likely as not to walk through an authorised red-light district on their way to school is very different. Yes, children can discuss sex during their primary school years, but it is discussed in an atmosphere of talking about relationships and caring and respect for others.

As Siebe Heutzepeter, headteacher of De Burght school in Amsterdam, puts it: 'The English are embarrassed to talk about sex. They are too squeamish. Here adults and children are better educated. It would be unthinkable for a Dutch parent to withdraw their child from sex education. I have only had one Muslim mother who left halfway through a parents' talk on sex.' He added: 'There is no point in telling children just to say "no" – this is a liberal country: you need to tell them why they are saying "no" and when to say "yes".'

Why is our sex education different?

The curriculum – even that proposed under the review – is more prescriptive. On the face of it, it looks as though it is presenting pupils with a number of facts rather than trying to encourage them to come to a deeper understanding of emotions. For instance, all children from the age of five will learn about body parts and animal reproduction; puberty and intercourse from the age of seven; and pregnancy, contraception and safer sex from the age of 11 when they have transferred to secondary school. However, the new curriculum will attempt to stop sex education being consigned to biology lessons ('now we have naming of parts' as it is often caricatured) and ensure that children learn about relationships and the option of abstinence along with the facts of life.

Does that suggest a will to learn from countries like Holland?

In launching the review, Schools Minister Jim Knight was careful to refer to the need for 'relationship education'. One of the reasons why the subject has been so poorly delivered in the past has been because there are not enough teachers trained to deliver it. In a secondary school, in particular, it would not be a favoured option for most teachers to volunteer to deliver a class on sex education to youngsters approaching or in their teens. The Government hopes to rectify this by providing and encouraging more teachers to become dedicated PSHE teachers by 2010.

Are the curriculum reforms likely to work?

That is hard to say. As educationists in Holland put it, it is as much about changing attitudes and culture in the UK as it is about developing lesson plans. Sanderjin van der Doef, an author of a series of books on sex education for use in Dutch schools, says: 'Here sex is a normal daily part of life, like shopping or football. In England it is a joke or a nudge.'

An example of the polarisation of views on Britain's recognition as the teenage pregnancy capital of western Europe can be seen from comments placed on a newspaper website recently asking what age children should be taught the facts of life following the publication of the Government review of the subject.

'I think it is a terrible idea to teach sex education to children aged five. Giving sex lessons to innocent children destroys their childhood,' said one

contributor. This view was backed up by another who added: 'Young uneducated unmarried girls are not having babies because of a lack of sex education.' This was counteracted by another contributor who argued: 'The Netherlands educates children about sex very early and has the lowest number of teenage pregnancies in Europe.' Another added: 'Children need facts, not ignorance.'

Should the UK learn from other countries?

Yes
⇨ Teenage pregnancy rates in the UK demand that we learn from those with much lower rates.
⇨ In the Netherlands, sex education is delivered in the context of learning about relationships, not biology.
⇨ The UK does not have enough teachers trained in the delivery of the subject to teach it effectively.

No
⇨ It is not the business of schools to teach children about sex – it should be left to the parents.
⇨ Lessons abroad touch on topics which would be viewed by some faith groups as inappropriate in class.
⇨ Better to educate parents about their responsibilities rather than change the curriculum.

17 February 2009

© The Independent

Girls as young as 12 having abortions every year

Abortions are being carried out on dozens of girls aged 12 and 13, according to official figures. By Laura Donnelly, Health Correspondent

More than 450 teenagers below the age of 14 terminated pregnancies between 2005 and 2008, including 23 girls aged 12, the statistics from the Department of Health disclosed. Over the same period, 52 teenagers terminated four or more pregnancies before they reached their 18th birthday, as the total number of 'repeat terminations' hit record levels across England and Wales.

Andrew Lansley, the shadow health secretary, described the statistics as evidence that Labour's policies on teenage pregnancy had failed. 'When you look at the cases of young girls having abortions repeatedly, this is not just tragic and disturbing, but totally unnecessary,' he said.

He said the Tories would introduce policies to promote support for teenagers, while advocating more targeted use of long-acting contraceptive injections for teenagers who had already had an abortion.

The Government data disclosed that 64,715 repeat abortions were carried out across all age groups last year — the highest level on record and a rise of 22 per cent in a decade. They included 46 women who terminated at least eight pregnancies.

A proposal to reduce the legal limit for termination for abortion from 24 weeks was defeated last year following a fierce parliamentary debate and the new figures showed a sharp rise in terminations after at least 26 weeks. There were 241 between 2005 and 2008, a rise of 16 per cent from the previous three years.

A Department of Health spokesman said the Government had invested almost £50 million in efforts to prevent teenage pregnancies and that the rates of abortions for teenagers as a whole had fallen by 4.5 per cent in the past year.

27 June 2009

© Telegraph Group Limited, London 2010

Pilot did not reduce teen pregnancies

Evaluation suggests youth scheme pilot did not reduce teenage pregnancies

An evaluation of a government-funded pilot scheme aimed at reducing teenage pregnancy, drug use and school exclusion suggests it did not reduce – and perhaps might have increased – pregnancies among participants, according to an article just published in the *British Medical Journal*.

The study found that young teenage girls who took part in the Young Person's Development Programme (YPDP) were more likely to become pregnant than girls in a matched comparison group who did not participate and instead were receiving other forms of youth support.

18 months after enrolment, 16 per cent of young women in YPDP became pregnant compared with six per cent of those in the comparison group. 58 per cent of YPDP young women said they had had a sexual experience versus 33 per cent of comparisons. In addition, 34 per cent of YPDP young women said they were likely to become teenage mothers against 24 per cent of comparisons. The researchers found no evidence for such effects among young men, or of effects on other health outcomes such as substance use.

The independent evaluation was commissioned by the Department of Health and carried out by researchers from the Institute of Education and the London School of Hygiene & Tropical Medicine. Over 2,300 young people took part in the programme, which ran from 2004 to 2007 and was aimed at young men and women aged 13 to 15 deemed by teachers and other professionals as at risk of teenage pregnancy, substance use and school exclusion.

The programme, partly informed by a successful New York initiative, involved work in 27 pilot areas and offered education, training and employment opportunities, life-skills, mentoring, volunteering, sexual health and substance misuse education, arts, sports and advice on accessing services. Participants were to be involved for one year.

While much of the work was of high quality and some young people showed significant personal progress during their time as participants, many received fewer than the intended six to ten hours per week of services, and provision varied greatly between sites. The work was intended to be in addition to normal schooling but in some sites, young people participated in the scheme instead of school.

Researcher Meg Wiggins (Institute of Education) says 'Our evaluation findings suggest that programmes aimed exclusively at young people at risk may bring them into contact with others more disposed to engage in risky behaviours – and therefore make them more likely to engage in these behaviours themselves.'

Researcher Chris Bonell (London School of Hygiene & Tropical Medicine) adds: 'We recommend that if policymakers do aim to develop other youth schemes targeting vulnerable young people, they take on board the lessons from our research, and test the schemes using randomised controlled trials.'

Note

This article refers to the *BMJ* paper *Health outcomes of youth development programme in England: prospective matched comparison study*, by Meg Wiggins, Chris Bonell, Mary Sawtell, Helen Austerberry, Helen Burchett, Elizabeth Allen, Vicki Strange. *BMJ*, 2009: 339; pp148-151. To read the paper, visit the *BMJ*'s website here: www.bmj.com/cgi/content/full/339/jul07_2/b2534
8 July 2009

⇨ The above information is reprinted with kind permission from the Institute of Education, London. Visit www.ioe.ac.uk for more.

© *Institute of Education, London*

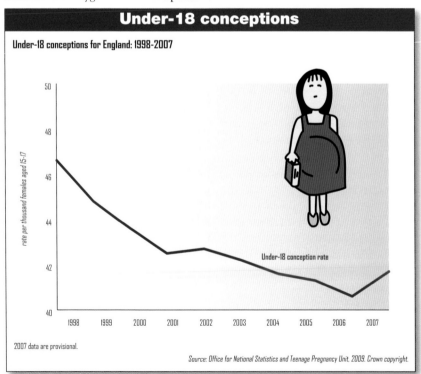

Under-18 conceptions

Under-18 conceptions for England: 1998-2007

rate per thousand females aged 15-17

Under-18 conception rate

2007 data are provisional.

Source: Office for National Statistics and Teenage Pregnancy Unit, 2009. Crown copyright.

School sex clinics could reduce teen pregnancy

Information from Medical News Today

Young people are more likely to use sexual health services if they can access them in schools, according to research being presented today at the Royal College of Nursing's 2009 International Research Conference in Cardiff.

Dr Debra Salmon, Reader in Community Health at the University of West England, will be presenting the evaluation of a pilot scheme which took place at 16 schools in the Neighbourhood Renewal Area of Bristol.

The nurse-led drop-in sexual health clinics proved popular with 'hard to reach' groups including boys and vulnerable young people who would not otherwise have received advice.

The evaluation reported high levels of satisfaction with the service and also found that young people are attending for information prior to their first sexual intercourse and were using the broad range of services provided, including contraception, STI testing and advice about relationships and delaying sex.

Commenting on the scheme, Dr Salmon said:

'61% of the young people we surveyed said they attended because it was at school and easy to access and that they would not have attended alternative provision. Providing convenient, accessible services is a great way of ensuring young people have access to the necessary sexual health advice.'

Dr Peter Carter, Chief Executive & General Secretary of the Royal College of Nursing (RCN), said:

'The role school nurses can play in reducing the shocking rate of teenage pregnancy and in raising awareness about sexual health issues cannot be underestimated. This evaluation provides further tangible evidence of the immense value they offer. It is crucial that sufficient funding is allocated to increase the numbers of school nurses if we are to beat the rising numbers of STIs and teenage pregnancies.'

27 March 2009

⇨ The above information is reprinted with kind permission from Medical News Today. Visit www.medicalnewstoday.com for more.

© *Medical News Today*

Education and pregnancy

Raising school leaving age could reduce teenage mothers

Making children leave school later could reduce the number of teenage mothers, according to new research by Sandra Black, Paul Devereux and Kjell Salvanes.

Their study, published in the July 2008 issue of *The Economic Journal*, suggests that this is because more educated teenage girls are less likely to become mothers, as well as because being in school longer reduces the time available to engage in risky behaviour.

The researchers analyse evidence from two countries: the United States and Norway. The former is much more punitive in its treatment of young mothers than Norway, which provides extensive financial support for teenagers with children.

But in both countries, increasing the compulsory school leaving age has reduced the incidence of teenage pregnancy.

Giving birth as a teenager normally has undesirable consequences for the young mother. On average, it means that girls are likely to leave school earlier, less likely to enter the job market and, even if they do so, they are likely to earn less.

We know that teenagers are less likely to become mothers the more educated they are. But until now, it was unclear whether forcing girls to stay in school longer would reduce the chance that they became mothers at a young age.

The report also sheds light on why raising the school leaving age has this effect. There are two ways it might work. The first is the 'incarceration effect': keeping teenagers in school reduces the opportunity for girls to become pregnant.

The second is the 'human capital effect': the more educated teenagers are, the higher their current and expected future human capital will be, which will make them less likely to have children at young ages.

The study suggests that both the incarceration effect and the human capital effect are important in reducing the incidence of teenage pregnancy.

With recent Government proposals to make schooling to 18 compulsory, the effects of extending the school leaving age are particularly pertinent to the UK. The country also has the highest rate of teenage pregnancy in Western Europe, according to a United Nations report published last year.

July 2008

⇨ The above information is reprinted with kind permission from the *Economic Journal*. Visit www.res.org.uk for more information.

© *The Economic Journal*

Sex education: why the British should go Dutch

Britain's Schools Minister plans to introduce sex lessons for five-year-olds. They already have them in the Netherlands. Is that why they also have the lowest teenage pregnancy rate in Europe?

The children of De Burght school in Amsterdam walk past the red-light district to their classrooms every day, past the 'Peep Shows, Live Girls', the risqué underwear shops and the newsagents selling teen magazines with free condoms. At school the five-year-olds play mummies and daddies in the playground knowing what their parents did in bed last night.

> ## Sex is everywhere in the Netherlands, yet the country has the lowest teenage pregnancy rate in the West and the lowest rates of sexually transmitted diseases among young people

Next year, 12-year-old Sasha explains to me, they will learn how to put a condom on a broomstick (she says this without a trace of embarrassment, just a polite smile). Across the city, nine-year-old Marcus, who lives in a beautiful 18th-century house on a canal, has been watching a cartoon showing him how to masturbate. His sister, 11, has been writing an essay on reproduction and knows that it is legal for two consenting 12-year-olds to make love. Her favourite magazine, *Girls*, gives advice on techniques in bed, and her parents sometimes allow her to stay up to see a baby being born on the birthing channel.

Then there is Yuri, 16, who explains to me in perfect English that 'anal sex hurts at the beginning but if you persevere it can be very pleasurable'. When I ask whether he

By Alice Thomson

is gay, he says 'no' but he has watched a documentary on the subject with his parents.

Sex is everywhere in the Netherlands, yet the country has the lowest teenage pregnancy rate in the West and the lowest rates of sexually transmitted diseases among young people. Now Britain, with almost the highest rate of teenage pregnancy in Europe – five times higher than the Netherlands – wants to emulate its success.

Ministers are planning to introduce compulsory sex and relationships lessons for children from the age of five by 2010. There will be a 'naming of parts' session in which children learn the correct words for vagina and testicles, and many will receive a sex education comic called *Let's Grow with Nisha and Joe*.

The Government has chosen the Dutch model rather than the Nordic way of tackling the subject of sex because the Netherlands, unlike Scandinavian nations, also manages to have one of the lowest abortion rates in Europe. In Britain, the

number of abortions performed on under-16s rose by ten per cent last year to 4,376.

So how do the Dutch do it? Siebe Heutzepeter, the headmaster of De Burght school, laughs at the idea that sex lessons are all children need to stop them becoming sexually active too young.

'We don't have formal sex education in primary schools,' he says. 'The children talk about sex when they feel like it and when they want an explanation. We treat sex as a healthy physical activity between two adults who are in love. Every year we have teachers who are pregnant or getting married, whether they are gay or straight, so it is a good way to talk about adult relationships.'

Heutzepeter says that the Dutch are more relaxed than Britons in every aspect of their lives. 'The English are embarrassed to talk about sex. They are too squeamish. Here adults and children are better educated. It would be unthinkable for a Dutch parent to withdraw their child from sex discussions. I have had only one Muslim mother who left halfway through a parents' talk on sex.'

He believes it is important to talk to children in a relaxed way about sex before they become self-conscious and embarrassed. 'It is all about self-respect,' he said. 'There is no point in telling children just to say "no" – this is a liberal country; you need to tell them why they are saying "no" and when to say "yes".'

A series of books by Sanderijn van der Doef provides Dutch children with all they could need to know about sex. The book for five-year-olds has pictures on the cover of toddlers kissing each other on the lips. Inside, children are told why their mothers have breasts and shave their armpits, how smiley-faced sperm travel, how human beings prefer to lie on top of each other but dogs mate from behind, and what their father's penis looks like. The book for 11-year-olds shows a girl examining her genitals in a mirror, and explains about periods and the pill.

Van der Doef is a star in her country and her manuals have become classics. Dutch parents read them to their children at bedtime, for information and enjoyment. 'Here sex is a normal daily part of life, like shopping or football. In England it is a joke,' says the author. 'My books teach children what adults do when they love each other and how babies are created. Children as young as four should know if they were born by Caesarean section or after artificial insemination. It is vital to be honest.'

John van der Woning, the head of one of Amsterdam's leading schools, Willemspark, says: 'We teach children about all sorts of sex. We have lots of homosexual teachers and they celebrated a marriage of two female teachers recently. But we also try to teach the older children about the darker side of sex, about prostitution and child abuse. It's important to be open about the world.'

At secondary school the sex education is formalised and children are shown how to use various types of contraceptive, how to have 'safe and pleasurable sex', the importance of responsibility and how to recognise the symptoms of sexually transmitted diseases.

This openness seems to work. In Britain the average teenager loses his or her virginity at 16 – more than a year before the Dutch average of 17.7 years. About 93 per cent of young people in the Netherlands use contraception, compared with 53 per cent in Britain. A study of teenagers in both countries found that while boys and girls in the Netherlands gave 'love and commitment' as the main reason for losing their virginity, boys in Britain cited peer pressure and physical attraction.

But Laura Watts, a British mother who has lived in the Netherlands for the past ten years, thinks that the lower rate of teenage pregnancy there may have more to do with family structure than with sex education. Dutch children are five times less likely to be living in a family headed by a lone parent, divorce rates are far lower and fewer mothers are in full-time employment.

Time to put an end to "the birds and the bees" euphemisms?

'I think my eight-year-old son has probably learnt more about sex from David Attenborough than from school,' she says. 'It is the family that makes the difference. Parents leave the office by 5pm in Holland and eat dinner with their children at 6pm. They then watch TV or play sport together, so they tend to be closer to their children and can guide them to do the right thing.'

Trudie, a fashion stylist, has always talked about sex with her daughter. When, at 16, her daughter asked her what sperm looked like, Trudie asked her husband to provide a sample. 'My daughter walks past sex shops every day, the family watches sex scenes together on television and we try to be as open as possible. It's not considered smutty, as it is in England.'

Henny de Barbarison, a teacher at De Burght school, agrees: 'My 18-year-old son still walks around the house naked – that's healthy. Everyone here is more relaxed.' Her female students are taught about 'lover boys' who flirt with girls just to have sex with them, then pressurise them to sleep with other members of their group. Male students are taught about homosexual sex. There are no 'no-go areas'.

'There is no point in telling children just to say "no" – this is a liberal country; you need to tell them why they are saying "no" and when to say "yes"'

Another reason why the teenage pregnancy rate is so low may be that in the Netherlands there is still a stigma attached to having a child before the age of 20. In Britain, a baby who can offer unconditional love, a free home away from parents and a cheque every month is not considered a disaster for a teenage girl. The Dutch Government still penalises single mothers under 18, who are expected to live with their parents if they become pregnant. Until six years ago the Government gave them no financial support.

Dutch children are taught that getting pregnant in their teens is a barrier to success. 'I'm not prepared to risk messing up my life. I am strong enough to wait,' says Ruby, 12. 'I want to be 19 and in love before I have sex,' says her friend Grace. Julia, 11, says: 'My mother's best friend is gay, my hairdresser is gay, half my family seem to be gay. It's not an issue.'

Children in their final year of primary school have not been shielded from anything, but their teachers have continually reinforced the message that sex is about love and commitment. The pupils all agree that they will not sleep with anyone until they have finished secondary school and are in a serious relationship.

Vanessa Storm de Grave, a mother of four who works part-time for a publishing company, thinks that her compatriots may be more responsible about sex than the British because the Netherlands is a more religious country. 'The family is very important here,' she says. 'Almost no mothers work full time; they see their main role as educating their children.

'I hope I will teach my eldest son how to become a responsible man by example, but I tell him anything he wants to know. I have talked about homosexuality and why it means that you can't have babies, but he is more interested in sport.'

Doortje Braeker, a Dutch mother who works in Britain for the International Planned Parenthood Federation, says: 'We are not scared of young people being sexually active and we want to make sure that their first experiences are safe and pleasurable. We are a Calvinist country so it is important that we don't have too many abortions, but the postwar generation also wants to have fun.'

Braeker was shocked when she first came to Britain. 'Young girls here seem to have babies to prove that they are adults. In the Netherlands it would just prove how uneducated and naive you are,' she says. 'There you can have a boy as a friend, here it's almost always about sex.'

Mena Laura Meyer, who produced the seven-part documentary series *Sexy* for Dutch TV last year, says that sex education is the least relevant aspect of the country's success. 'All the children I talked to were quite dismissive about their sex education at school,' she says. 'They appreciated knowing how to put on a condom but were more interested in the emotional than the physical side of sex.'

Her series, which addressed every issue from anal sex to S&M, was watched by more than a quarter of Dutch households. 'All you watch in Britain are your soaps, which are all about single mums, and your wildlife documentaries, which just cover penguins mating,' she says. 'Sex and relationships aren't government issues. Until the British can sit down together and watch programmes about masturbation and birth, you will never have a healthy attitude to sex.'

In Britain the Government has decided that schools must bear responsibility for sex education. Jim Knight, the Schools Minister, insists that from 2010 schools must make time for the new personal, social and health education (PSHE) syllabus. Children aged five to seven will learn about feelings; those aged eight to 11 will be taught about the biological aspects of sex. At secondary school they will learn about contraception and sexually transmitted diseases.

But maybe it's up to parents. Perhaps we should all be buying our toddlers *Mummy Laid An Egg* by Babette Cole, leaving condoms around the house, as one Dutch mother suggests, 'to prompt discussions', and sitting down to supper each evening to discuss our relationships.

One colleague attempted this, and her 12-year-old son asked her 'how many positions are there?' in front of the babysitter. My eight-year-old asked me if it was more painful to wax my legs than to give birth.

But after my few days in the Netherlands, my children now understand where babies come from. It has marred the beginning of *Dumbo* when the storks come down from the clouds, but I hope it will turn them into more responsible adults.

Maybe, instead of expecting schools to teach children morality and the missionary position, the British should adopt a few other Dutch lessons. Employers could encourage staff to go home at 5pm for a family supper, parents could discuss contraception with their children, and the BBC could ask David Attenborough to turn his attention to human reproduction.

24 November 2008

© *The Times, 2010*

Everyday conversations, every day

Executive summary

We live in challenging times. Parenting can be both fun and rewarding, as well as difficult and disempowering on a number of levels. Intense peer and media pressures introduce sexual knowledge at an ever younger age; new technology drives teen communication; and a culture of conspicuous consumption reigns from the young teens upwards.[1] These are just some of the reasons why parents can feel they are losing connection and influence with their young sons and daughters.

Amidst all of this, headlines don't help and would have us believe that teens are in turmoil – getting pregnant and having sex too young, indulging in criminal behaviour, taking drugs and binge drinking: parents are rendered fearful. Alongside this, anxiety is rife that teens don't want to talk, and even if they do, worries persist that parents talking about sex is akin to encouragement.

The *Everyday Conversations, Every Day* report pulls together in one place the learning of 14 academic, professional and governmental studies. These provided hypotheses that were put to the test by new attitudinal research amongst 1,000 parents and teens. In the report, Anita Naik draws on over 17 years' experience as a professional teen agony aunt and parenting author. This role has uniquely equipped her to understand the pressures on today's teens and to generate sensitive and practical solutions to common problems.

The report is arranged in five sections addressing parental fears, when, who and how to talk and culminates with a set of tested tips on how to discuss sex and relationships in families. The insights it generates make for compelling and frequently surprising reading. Significant evidence shows that parents can counter risky behaviour, particularly when it comes to sex.

British teens are eager to talk – 75% of 11- to 14-year-olds want, but currently find it difficult, to talk about sex and relationships with their parents. A resounding 99% feel talking wouldn't encourage them to have sex as many parents fear.[2]

Intense peer and media pressures introduce sexual knowledge at an ever younger age

---

Despite this, over half of parents (55%) hold back due to embarrassment because they don't know how to start.[3] Talking to teens can help them make responsible choices about sex and sexual health. If parents can cross the generational divide and instigate conversations, they will help teens:
⇨ understand sex;
⇨ handle peer pressure;

⇨ limit risky behaviour.

Empowering teens in this way not only helps reduce the teen pregnancy rate, but delays early sex and helps teens protect themselves from pregnancy and sexually transmitted infections when they do start having sex.

A review of recent research shows the guiding principle to improve teen/parent relationships lies in parents having everyday conversations, every day with teens, to help normalise the subject of sex and sexual health. Talking, listening and taking an active interest in the teen's life not only helps bring parents and teens closer for the long term, but it also helps parents to feel they are doing a better job.

Approached in the right way, it has been proven that parent-teen talking can have a positive impact on the confidence and actions of teens, as well as help reduce the unplanned and unwanted teenage pregnancies that occur every year.[4]

In fact, one of the many reasons why the Netherlands and Scandinavia have been so successful in reducing their teenage pregnancy rates is because parents in these countries talk more openly to their children about sex and relationships from a young age.

Through talking, parents can reverse the power shift they sense as a result of technological and other advances and the growing influence of their teens' peers, which they feel has alienated them from their teens. Achieving this can help ensure not only that accuracy prevails when it comes to sex and sexual health but that teens are given a lifeline to the world that leaves them better prepared and ready to take responsibility.

Notes

1 *Information Needs of Parents on Sensitive Subjects Research* commissioned by Tina Trythall, COI on behalf of the Department for Children, Schools and Families, May 2008
2 Populus, June 2008
3 Populus, June 2008
4 *Young People, Substance Misuse and Sexual Behaviour*, Adfam/MPRC report 2006
June 2008

⇨ The above information is an extract from the report *Everyday Conversations, Every Day* and is reprinted with kind permission from Parents Centre. Visit www.parentscentre.gov.uk for more information.

© *Crown copyright*

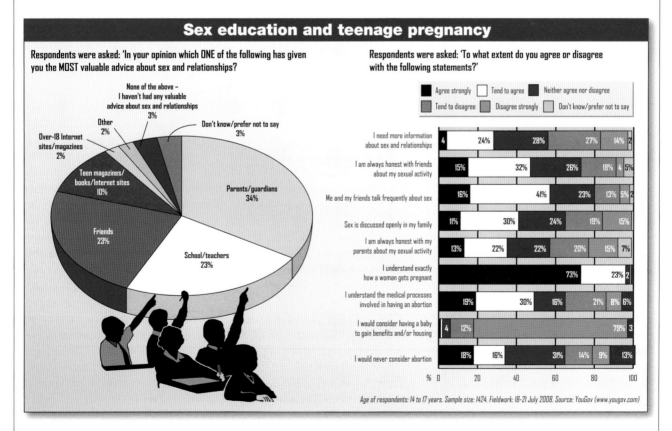

Sex education and teenage pregnancy

Respondents were asked: 'In your opinion which ONE of the following has given you the MOST valuable advice about sex and relationships?'

- None of the above – I haven't had any valuable advice about sex and relationships 3%
- Other 2%
- Over-18 Internet sites/magazines 2%
- Teen magazines/books/Internet sites 10%
- Friends 23%
- School/teachers 23%
- Parents/guardians 34%
- Don't know/prefer not to say 3%

Respondents were asked: 'To what extent do you agree or disagree with the following statements?'

Legend: Agree strongly / Tend to agree / Neither agree nor disagree / Tend to disagree / Disagree strongly / Don't know/prefer not to say

- I need more information about sex and relationships: 4, 24%, 28%, 27%, 14%, 2
- I am always honest with friends about my sexual activity: 15%, 32%, 26%, 18%, 4, 5%
- Me and my friends talk frequently about sex: 16%, 41%, 23%, 13%, 5%, 2
- Sex is discussed openly in my family: 11%, 30%, 24%, 19%, 15%
- I am always honest with my parents about my sexual activity: 13%, 22%, 22%, 20%, 15%, 7%
- I understand exactly how a woman gets pregnant: 73%, 23%, 2
- I understand the medical processes involved in having an abortion: 19%, 30%, 16%, 21%, 8%, 6%
- I would consider having a baby to gain benefits and/or housing: 4, 12%, 79%, 3
- I would never consider abortion: 18%, 16%, 31%, 14%, 9%, 13%

% 0 20 40 60 80 100

Age of respondents: 14 to 17 years. Sample size: 1424. Fieldwork: 18-21 July 2008. Source: YouGov (www.yougov.com)

We're in a state of sexual confusion

The line has blurred between information and tacit encouragement, argues Jenny McCartney

Since this Government came to power, one of its most frequently and piously declared goals has been to reduce the number of teenage pregnancies. It has thus poured more than £280 million of taxpayers' money into contraception services and sex education in the last decade, not least because it calculates that teenage mothers tend to cost the state even more after they give birth.

The latest dismal figures, however, showed the rate of pregnancy among under-16s at its highest for ten years. The Government responded by vowing a further £20 million to policies which include long-term contraceptive injections and implants for teenagers. It was also suggested last week that abortion clinics should be allowed to advertise on television and advertisements for condoms be routinely screened before the nine o'clock watershed. Apart from the inherent distastefulness of such initiatives, there is little likelihood that they will work. The Government has taken on the aspect of a dead-eyed Las Vegas gambler, slumped at the roulette wheel, throwing good money and principles after bad.

It has been confusedly reported that the suggestion to televise advertisements for abortion clinics is an effort to 'curb teenage pregnancies'. This is not true, since an abortion clinic can only be of interest when pregnancy has already occurred. It is in fact an effort to curb live births to teenage mothers.

There is a grotesque and widening gulf in how society depicts pregnancy in mothers of different ages and classes. The pregnancy of an older, middle-class mother – a triumph over the dreaded spectre of infertility – or a wealthy celebrity is increasingly viewed by the media as a miraculous event: the world is beckoned in to relish vicariously everything from the first perceptible flutterings of foetal limbs to the gloriously expanding size of the bump.

If a 14-year-old girl should fall pregnant, however, sentimental cooing is replaced by cold functionality. The official line from the top down is: quick, get the damn thing 'sorted out'. If she agrees, the bemused girl is rushed to the nearest clinic for a termination, after which she is generally supposed to shut up about it and hug her shameful little secret close. Some girls may bounce back from such an experience with relative insouciance, others may find that it haunts them psychologically ever after. Responses to abortion are deep-rooted, complicated and rarely discussed in public: it's the sorrowful, silent side of sex.

I am not opposed to the provision of abortion services, sex education or contraception. I am, however, opposed to the persistent trivialising of both abortion and sex, particularly with regard to adolescents. The Government's policy of constant nagging about contraception has not solved the problem of teenage conception at all: it has made it worse. The line has been blurred between information and tacit encouragement.

Imagine that you are a 14-year-old British girl, growing up in a society saturated in the notion that women should do whatever it takes to make themselves attractive to men. You acquire a 15-year-old boyfriend whom you're eager to keep, and he starts pressuring you to have sex. You feel uneasy, yet sex is precisely what society seems to expect of you. For years, you've been bombarded with detail on sex, contraception, and the morning-after pill, and repeatedly informed that there's no need to feel guilty so long as you're 'responsible'. You know this, and your boyfriend does too. But the bottom line is that if you should end up pregnant, suddenly the easy-going quasi-approval stops: you're still dumped on your own in a lonely place, outside the abortion clinic or the antenatal ward.

It's time we stopped telling teenagers lies, that sex is inherently carefree, contraception infallible, abortion a casual technical procedure. Yet these are precisely the myths that the Government's escalating strategy seems designed to promote, at the same time as effectively dangling early motherhood as a state-subsidised career option to those with few other prospects. On current form, no one should be surprised if, ten years hence, our politicians are still poring over the teenage pregnancy statistics and wondering where it all went wrong.

28 March 2009

© *Telegraph Group Limited, London 2010*

Teenage pregnancy: mothers' tide

A ten-year strategy has seen a reversal of the once surging rate of teenage pregnancy in many areas – but in others the numbers of teens choosing to have a baby remain alarming

⇨ *England's under-18 pregnancy rate has fallen nearly 13 per cent since 1999 but remains high in some areas.*
⇨ *Social marketing is being used to understand cultural factors.*
⇨ *Risks to teenage mothers include poor antenatal care and higher infant mortality rates.*

By Claire Measures

It has become apparent over the past ten years that reducing the rates of teenage pregnancy in England cannot be achieved by a single agency. Not just a health problem for the NHS to solve, the issue requires the involvement of social services, education, local communities, parents and teenagers themselves.

There is still a long way to go if England is to achieve the targets set by the 1999 teenage pregnancy strategy, namely, to reduce the rate of under-18 conceptions by half by 2010 and to get more teenage parents into education, training or employment, to reduce their risk of long-term social exclusion. Devolved government means the strategy refers only to England, although the issues around teenage pregnancy are similar in the other UK nations.

At the strategy's launch, the under-18 conception rate in England was 44.8 per 1,000. It has come down 12.6 per cent since then and by 2006 was at its lowest level for 20 years. Latest figures for 2007 show a slight increase for the first time since 2002, from 40.9 per 1,000 to 41.9 per 1,000.

The target for 2010 remains a long way off. Overall, 89 per cent of local areas have achieved reductions in teenage pregnancy rates compared with their 1998 baseline. Around 20 per cent have achieved reductions of over 25 per cent, including Hackney (down by 25.9 per cent) and Oldham (down by 29.4 per cent).

At the strategy's launch, the under-18 conception rate in England was 44.8 per 1,000. It has come down 12.6 per cent since then and by 2006 was at its lowest level for 20 years

'Teenage pregnancy is a complex issue which requires a multifaceted approach. While some areas are on trajectory for their local 2010 target, progress towards the national 50 per cent reduction is challenging and it has taken other countries 30 years to bring the rates down,' says a spokesperson for the Department for Children, Schools and Families, where the Government's teenage pregnancy unit is housed.

Those that have succeeded include the Netherlands and Scandinavian countries, which have been held up as examples of how to grasp the socio-sexual revolution and equip young people to deal with it by promoting sex education and contraceptive advice, as well as regarding teenage sexuality with respect. The UK, meanwhile, has long been berated for having the 'highest teenage pregnancy rate in Europe', while the US has the highest rate among English-speaking countries.

'When you talk to the countries which have got this more right than us, they say "we really respect and value young people's sexuality. We want them to have sex lives that are positive, rewarding and exciting and we tell them that and we state our expectations of them." Here, at best, we are ambivalent about young people's sexuality,' says Simon Blake, chief executive of young people's sexual health charity Brook.

Teenage pregnancy risks

Teenage pregnancy is considered a poor choice on both health and social grounds. Teenage parents tend to have poor antenatal health, lower birth weight babies, higher infant mortality rates and an increased risk of congenital anomalies.

Likely to seek antenatal care much later in pregnancy than older women, teenage mothers miss out on important preconception and early pregnancy health measures, such as taking folic acid. Teenage mothers are less likely to breastfeed their babies than older mothers and are more likely, if from a deprived background, to remain poor and to experience higher levels of unemployment. They are also disproportionately likely to suffer relationship breakdown.

However, for some young women, having a baby is seen as a positive step, one that offers a sense of purpose in a life that might have few other options.

It is towards this group of women that teenage pregnancy teams are directing their greatest efforts.

In 2006, the Department for Children, Schools and Families published a next steps document, after a 'deep dive' review in 2005 of three high performing local authorities and three with static or increasing rates, looking at what was and what was not working in reducing teenage pregnancy rates.

Since then, the unit has focused closely on 21 areas with high and increasing teenage pregnancy rates, with the teenage pregnancy national support team being sent in to examine local issues and advise on best practice. Important in such work is joint working that starts at the top, with senior representation from agencies including the primary care trust, the local authority, and voluntary sector organisations on a teenage pregnancy partnership board. In addition, work has to be incorporated into the local Primary Care Trust (PCT) and local authority children and young people plan.

Bristol and Wigan are just two of the 'hotspot' areas where teenage pregnancy figures have failed to come down in the last ten years. The most recent data available showed Bristol had a rate of 54.7 pregnancies per 1,000 girls aged 15 to 17. In Wigan the rate was 53.9 per 1,000.

Bristol teaching PCT associate director of public health Barbara Coleman acknowledges the city has been slower than other areas in adopting partnership working and believes this may have contributed to Bristol's near static teenage pregnancy rate.

In Wigan, council teenage pregnancy co-ordinator Eleanor Mansell has high hopes that an extensive restructuring of teenage pregnancy management will co-ordinate efforts more effectively.

'A 50 per cent reduction target by 2010 is extremely challenging,' she says. The director of public health is a joint post across the local authority and PCT, while joint posts below that will line manage teenage pregnancy.

The area has also developed the 'You're Welcome' initiative, which sets down guidelines for healthcare organisations providing services to young people, increases access to contraception and sexual health services and provides health services in secondary schools.

Bristol has an outreach teenage health service in virtually every secondary school – a pattern repeated in most local authorities.

'The outreach service in schools and other settings is linked with Brook. We have got the service in almost every senior school, which means that young people who want access to sexual health services and contraception can do so as well as being signposted to mainstream health services,' says Ms Coleman.

Arsenal of prevention

Also common are condom distribution schemes such as the C card, a card that young people can produce at places such as clinics and youth centres, to be given free condoms.

Long-acting reversible contraceptives are another key component in the arsenal of prevention but as they are historically surrounded by myths (that their use causes weight gain or can impair fertility), PCTs have their work cut out promoting their benefits to young people.

And the time lag for the reporting of conception statistics is lengthy due to the nine months of pregnancy plus the time it takes to register a birth and the time it takes for that statistic to appear in Office of National Statistics records, so it is difficult to evaluate the effectiveness of any service in reducing teenage pregnancy, especially in the short term.

'We started with one of the highest rates in the UK so our trajectory was a lot steeper than many other PCTs.' So far we have seen quite a dramatic reduction – a drop of 28 per cent from the 1998 figures of around 77 per 1,000 to around 56 per 1,000. Our target for 2010 is around 31.8 per 1,000 so we need to double what we have achieved so far,' says Hackney and City PCT deputy director of public health Jose Figueroa.

'We tried to commission two evaluations but it is probably quite ambitious to do something like that. For instance, sex and relationships education is provided through different routes – peer education, healthcare staff or theatre groups in schools. So far, we can see they are all complementing each other but what proportion of the impact should be allocated to each is very difficult to say.'

Known risk factors for teenage pregnancy are deprivation, poverty and poor educational attainment. In addition, the daughters of teenage mothers are twice as likely to become teenage mothers themselves. But while reducing health inequalities and providing accessible contraceptive and sexual health services are very much the remit of the NHS, what of dealing with the cultural issues embedded in communities that choose to have babies early?

'What we have struggled with for a number of years is this issue of why young people are choosing to take this route,' says Ms Coleman. 'It's not just about access to services and taking the prevention route. It's about aspirations. In some areas there are cultural silos where getting pregnant and having a baby is the thing to do.'

The problem is similar in Wigan.

'Our own research shows a cultural acceptance of teenage pregnancy in Wigan,' says Ms Mansell. The PCT is now focusing on understanding the local picture behind the data and the reality of life in those areas where teenage pregnancy is the choice of local girls.

However, Dr Figueroa says: 'I don't think it is the role of the PCT to change culture unless the impact on health is really negative.'

After an audit of teenage pregnancy in Hackney showed a disproportionate number among black teenagers (black African and black Caribbean) and 'white other' teenagers, more work was put into increasing access to sex and relationships education and contraception.

'We need the right kind of services for each community,' adds Dr Figueroa.

City and Hackney PCT has also launched a new sexual health website, www.sho-me.nhs.uk, which Dr Figueroa describes as 'about sex rather than being sexual'. Within a month of its launch, the site had received more than 500 hits, including genuine questions pouring into 'Dr Sarah', the site's medical advice service.

In Rotherham, where the teenage pregnancy rate is 50.7 per 1,000 15- to 17-year-old girls, local teenage pregnancy co-ordinator Melanie Simmonds says a scheme that began in 2006 in Maltby, an area of high teenage pregnancy, has enjoyed considerable success. The project helps young women make positive life choices and, of the 96 supported so far, only one became pregnant in the first year.

Now set to be rolled out to other areas of high teenage pregnancy in the town, the early intervention teams sit alongside children and young people's teams, with access to support from the police, youth inclusion workers and Connexions and senior youth workers.

'This is an exciting area of work that we are very proud of. Not only does it help the girls to be aware of safe sex and contraception, it supports them to build their self confidence, make friends, develop respect for themselves and others and make positive choices about their lives,' says Ms Simmonds.

The spokesperson for the Department for Children, Schools and Families says: 'Making progress requires changing young people's knowledge, attitudes and behaviour.

'We know that good local delivery can impact on rates, even in areas with high levels of deprivation and ingrained culture that young parenthood is inevitable.'

Targeted messages

Social marketing has proved central to understanding how to reach young people.

Wigan is launching a social marketing campaign 'to inform our delivery and look at all aspects of our young people and what they think', says Ms Mansell.

Such techniques have also played a key role at City and Hackney PCT.

'Social marketing makes sure everything we do is adequately targeted and involves members of the specific community. We used social marketing to increase awareness of the availability of information and

to empower young people to make informed decisions about when to start their sex lives and when to say no, if they want to say no,' says Dr Figueroa.

Ms Simmonds echoes this approach in Rotherham, where they are running a social marketing campaign around long-acting reversible contraception.

'We hope to empower Rotherham women, in particular young women, to make informed choices about their method of contraception by gaining an understanding both of the barriers and of the motivating factors to using it.'

But raising the aspirations of young people is arguably the most vital step in reducing UK teenage pregnancy rates.

'Ambition is the best form of contraception' is the mantra on the lips of those who work in the field and teenage pregnancy team.

Raising aspirations is also important for teenage parents. In one such move, Wigan has managed to reduce the rate of second pregnancies among teenagers.

'Wigan does exceptionally well in supporting teenage parents. We have very low repeat rates or repeat abortion rates. We are trying to use some of these techniques to wrap around vulnerable teenagers to support them before they get pregnant,' says Ms Mansell.

Peer support for young parents

Getting more teenage parents into education, training or employment to reduce their risk of long-term social exclusion was the second of the main targets of the 1999 teenage pregnancy strategy.

A peer-mentoring training scheme in Rotherham run by young women's support service Grow and children's charity Barnardo's was launched in April 2007.

The project aims to provide teenage parents and parents-to-be with a peer mentor and give them an opportunity to gain voluntary work experience.

Rotherham teenage pregnancy co-ordinator Melanie Simmonds says: 'The peer-mentoring training has empowered the girls. It gives them such a sense of achievement to know that they can help other young mums who may feel isolated and unsure of what services are available.'

Sharon Riley, who has just completed the mentor-accredited training, says: 'I did the course because I want to be able to help other young mums who are in a similar situation to me.

'I like helping people and hope to go on to do a counselling course.'
19 March 2009

⇨ This first appeared in *Health Service Journal*, 2009. Visit www.hsj.co.uk for more information.

© *Health Service Journal*

⇨ Less than one in ten men and women aged 16 to 44 surveyed had used no contraception at all when they first had sex. (page 1)

⇨ The UK has the highest teenage birth and abortion rates in Western Europe. (page 2)

⇨ The under-16 conception rate increased from 7.8 per 1,000 girls aged 13 to 15 in 2006 to 8.3 in 2007. There were an estimated 8,196 conceptions to girls aged under 16 in 2007, representing just under one per cent of all conceptions. (page 3)

⇨ The probability of becoming pregnant is highest around the time of ovulation (when the egg is released), when, on average, up to one third of women will become pregnant from having sex once. (page 4)

⇨ Funding up to the value of £160 per week is available, up to age 20, to enable young parents to continue their education at school and if they go on to college. (page 6)

⇨ Between 1998 and 2007 the teenage conception rate fell by 10.7 per cent in under-18s and by 6.4 per cent in under-16s. (page 7)

⇨ Babies to teenage mums tend to have a lower than average birth weight. Infant mortality is 60% higher than for babies of older women. (page 11)

⇨ 95% of people over-estimate the rate of under-16s who get pregnant each year and the same amount are unaware of the significant drop in this figure over the last decade. (page 13)

⇨ Unexpected pregnancies aren't a problem unique to young mums – around 40% of women have unplanned pregnancies. (page 15)

⇨ In 1970, young women aged 15 to 19 in England and Wales were almost twice as likely to become mums as they are today. (page 16)

⇨ The combined pill is over 99% effective in preventing pregnancies if taken regularly. (page 19)

⇨ The pill is highly effective and with perfect use has a failure rate of only 0.3% in the first year. But in practice, failure is much higher – closer to 8% or 9%. (page 21)

⇨ Rates of teenage motherhood in the UK, at 15%, are around twice those of Germany (8%), three times those of France (6%), and almost four times those of Sweden (4%). (page 22)

⇨ Among under-25s, only 37% use emergency contraception on every occasion that they have unprotected intercourse. (page 23)

⇨ Around 80% of under-18 conceptions are in 16- and 17-year-olds, which is the age most young people become sexually active. (page 24)

⇨ Teenage mothers are three times more likely to suffer from post-natal depression and experience poor mental health for up to three years after the birth. (page 27)

⇨ The teenage pregnancy rate in Holland is only one-fifth as high as that of the UK – only five births per 1,000 teenagers compared to the UK's 27. Its abortion rate per teenage head of the population is also one of the lowest in Europe. (page 28)

⇨ More than 450 teenagers below the age of 14 terminated pregnancies between 2005 and 2008, including 23 girls aged 12, statistics from the Department of Health disclosed. (page 29)

⇨ Young people are more likely to use sexual health services if they can access them in schools, according to research. (page 31)

⇨ Making children leave school later could reduce the number of teenage mothers, according to new research. (page 31)

⇨ Ministers are planning to introduce compulsory sex and relationships lessons for children from the age of five by 2010. There will be a 'naming of parts' session in which children learn the correct words for vagina and testicles, and many will receive a sex education comic called *Let's Grow with Nisha and Joe*. (page 32)

⇨ 75% of 11- to 14-year-olds want, but currently find it difficult, to talk about sex and relationships with their parents. A resounding 99% feel talking wouldn't encourage them to have sex as many parents fear. (page 35)

⇨ 34% of young people surveyed said that their parents/ guardians had been their most valuable source of information about sex and relationships. (page 35)

⇨ Teenage mothers are likely to seek antenatal care much later in pregnancy than older women. They are less likely to breastfeed their babies than older mothers and are more likely, if from a deprived background, to remain poor and to experience higher levels of unemployment. They are also disproportionately likely to suffer relationship breakdown. (page 37)

Abortion

The artificial ending of a pregnancy before it has reached full term. In England, Wales and Scotland, the law says this must take place before the 24th week of pregnancy. In Northern Ireland, abortion is legal only in exceptional circumstances. 20,289 women aged under 18 had an abortion in England and Wales in 2007.

Age of consent

The age at which an individual can legally take part in sexual intercourse. In the UK, the age of consent to any form of sexual activity is 16 for both men and women, whether they are heterosexual, homosexual or bisexual.

The Alfie Patten case

In February 2009, the *Sun* newspaper ran a story about a boy named Alfie Patten, who, it was claimed, had become a parent at the age of 13 with his 15-year-old girlfriend. The case caused widespread consternation in the media and among politicians, and triggered debate about teenage sexual behaviour and the effectiveness of sex and relationships education. However, in May 2009 a DNA test revealed that Alfie was not the baby's father.

Bisexual

A person is said to be bisexual, or 'bi', if they have intercourse and form relationships with people of either sex.

Conception

When a female egg is fertilised by a male sperm; the beginning of a pregnancy.

Contraception

Contraception is used during sexual intercourse to prevent pregnancy. Barrier methods such as condoms are also effective in preventing most sexually transmitted infections. The most common types of contraception are condoms and 'the pill' (the combined or mini contraceptive pill). Emergency contraception such as the 'morning-after pill' can also be used for a limited period after sex to prevent a pregnancy.

Heterosexual

A person is said to be heterosexual, or 'straight', if they have intercourse and form relationships with people of the opposite sex.

Homosexual

A person is said to be homosexual, or 'gay', if they have intercourse and form relationships with people of the same sex.

Sex and relationships education (SRE)

Sex and relationships education takes place in schools; its purpose is to help young people acquire information and form attitudes about sex, sexual identity, relationships and intimacy, so that they can make informed decisions about their own sexual activities and avoid unwanted outcomes such as unplanned pregnancy or catching sexually transmitted infections. The Government announced in October 2008 that SRE was to be made a compulsory part of the national curriculum in primary and secondary schools in an effort to tackle teenage pregnancy and the spread of sexually transmitted infections.

Sexual intercourse

When the erect male penis is inserted into the female vagina, this is called sex or sexual intercourse. Semen containing sperm is released during intercourse, and if no contraception is used, a male sperm can join with the female egg to cause pregnancy.

INDEX

Additional Resources

Other Issues titles

If you are interested in researching further some of the issues raised in *Teenage Conceptions*, you may like to read the following titles in the **Issues** series:

⇨ Vol. 176 *Health Issues for Young People* (ISBN 978 1 86168 500 1)

⇨ Vol. 173 *Sexual Health* (ISBN 978 1 86168 487 5)

⇨ Vol. 171 *Abortion – Rights and Ethics* (ISBN 978 1 86168 485 1)

⇨ Vol. 166 *Marriage and Cohabitation* (ISBN 978 1 86168 470 7)

⇨ Vol. 164 *The AIDS Crisis* (ISBN 978 1 86168 468 4)

⇨ Vol. 160 *Poverty and Exclusion* (ISBN 978 1 86168 453 0)

⇨ Vol. 124 *Parenting Issues* (ISBN 978 1 86168 363 2)

For more information about these titles, visit our website at www.independence.co.uk/publicationslist

Useful organisations

You may find the websites of the following organisations useful for further research:

⇨ **AVERT:** www.avert.org

⇨ **Brook:** www.brook.org.uk

⇨ **Chris Bryant MP:** www.teenagemums.org.uk

⇨ **Connexions 360:** www.connexions360.org.uk

⇨ **Department for Children, Schools and Families:** www.dcsf.gov.uk

⇨ **Education for Choice:** www.efc.org.uk

⇨ **fpa:** www.fpa.org.uk

⇨ **Healthy Respect:** www.healthyrespect.co.uk

⇨ **NHS Choices:** www.nhs.co.uk

⇨ **Office for National Statistics:** www.statistics.gov.uk

⇨ **Parents Centre:** www.parentscentre.gov.uk

⇨ **TheSite:** www.thesite.org

⇨ **Youngdads:** www.youngdads.co.uk

⇨ **YWCA:** www.ywca.org.uk

ACKNOWLEDGEMENTS

The publisher is grateful for permission to reproduce the following material.

While every care has been taken to trace and acknowledge copyright, the publisher tenders its apology for any accidental infringement or where copyright has proved untraceable. The publisher would be pleased to come to a suitable arrangement in any such case with the rightful owner.

Chapter One: Teenage Pregnancy

Teenagers: sexual behaviour and pregnancy, © **fpa**, Conception rate increases among under-18s, © Crown copyright is reproduced with the permission of Her Majesty's Stationery Office, Frequently asked questions about pregnancy, © AVERT, Teenage pregnancy, © East Sussex County Council, Teenage pregnancy facts, © **fpa**, Making a decision, © Education for Choice, The worst in Europe, © Chris Bryant MP, It takes two to make a teenage pregnancy, © Guardian Newspapers Limited 2010, How many teens get pregnant? © Brook.

Chapter Two: Young Parents

Parenthood?, © Education for Choice, Young mums, © TheSite.org, Young mums: the real story, © YWCA, Justin's story, © Youngdads.co.uk, Supervised homes for young mums, © Guardian Newspapers Limited 2010, Supporting teenage mums, © Guardian Newspapers Limited 2010.

Chapter Three: Solutions

Condoms and contraception, © Healthy Respect® is a registered trademark of the Lothian Health Board (2009), Condoms: know the facts, © Crown copyright is reproduced with the permission of Her Majesty's Stationery Office, Should the pill be available without prescription? Yes, © BMJ Publishing Group, Should the pill be available without prescription? No, © BMJ Publishing Group, Contraception and teenage pregnancy, © Crown copyright is reproduced with the permission of Her Majesty's Stationery Office, More cash for contraception, © Crown copyright is reproduced with the permission of Her Majesty's Stationery Office, About the Teenage Pregnancy Strategy, © Crown copyright is reproduced with the permission of Her Majesty's Stationery Office, The big question, © The Independent, Girls as young as 12 having abortions every year, © Telegraph Group Ltd, London 2010, Pilot did not reduce teen pregnancies, © Institute of Education, London, School sex clinics could reduce teen pregnancy, © Medical News Today, Education and pregnancy, © The Economic Journal, Sex education: why the British should go Dutch, © The Times, 2010, Everyday conversations, every day, © Crown copyright is reproduced with the permission of Her Majesty's Stationery Office, We're in a state of sexual confusion, © Telegraph Group Limited, London 2010, Teenage pregnancy: mothers' tide, © Health Service Journal.

Photographs

Flickr: page 8 (Nate Grigg).
Stock Xchng: pages 9 (Benjamin Earwicker); 13 (Matthew Bowden); 17 (Vivek Chugh); 20 (Lotus Head); 24 (Tijmen van Dobbenburgh); 27 (Sanja Gjenero).
Wikimedia Commons: page 33 (Fir0002, Noodle snacks).

Illustrations

Pages 2, 11, 21, 32: Don Hatcher; pages 4, 12, 23, 36: Simon Kneebone; pages 6, 15, 26, 39: Angelo Madrid; pages 7, 14: Bev Aisbett.

And with thanks to the team: Mary Chapman, Sandra Dennis, Claire Owen and Jan Sunderland.

Lisa Firth
Cambridge
January, 2010